Rescue
The
Captors
2

Russell Stendal

Rescue the Captors II
© 2008 Russell M. Stendal
All Rights Reserved.

ISBN 0-931221-61-7

Ransom Press International
10160 Main Dr.
Bonita Springs, Fla. 34135

Printed in Colombia
May, 2013

Table Of Contents

Map of Colombia

Kogi Indians

Site of Pacho's Kidnapping

Bogota

Meta

The Mountain

San Martín

Chaparral

Lomalinda

Caño Jabon

Puerto Toledo

To Noel

Preface

Russell Martin Stendal was born on November 25, 1955 in Minneapolis, MN., the son of a prominent civil engineer. He prayed when he was only 4 years old that God would send his parents to the mission field so that he wouldn't have to wait till he grew up to be a missionary. By the time he was eight, the Lord had answered his prayer. After a miraculous turn of events, he was on his way to Colombia, South America, with his parents and two younger siblings.

The family was soon called to work with a small, almost unknown tribe high in the Colombian Sierra Nevada Mountains. The Stendals spent many years working with the Kogi tribe, helping with medical needs and translating the New Testament into their language. Russell and his siblings enthusiastically helped their parents with everything that needed to be done to accomplish this arduous task, keeping up their studies by home school. After much prayer and difficulty, the Kogi leaders, people who had never welcomed strangers and who never had any contact with the outside world, not only allowed them to live in their village, but allowed civil engineer, Chad Stendal, to build a small airstrip so he could fly medical supplies and food up to the village. It was while watching the first plane land up in the tiny, hidden airstrip his father built high up in the almost impossible terrain of the Sierra Nevada Mountains, that Russell first discovered that he wanted to become a pilot.

By the time Russell was in his early twenties, he had become an expert jungle pilot, married a beautiful Colombian girl named Marina, and had settled down in eastern Colombia. During the late seventies, this area was beginning to see itself influenced and contaminated by the drug trafficking industry that would soon spread like wild fire throughout the entire country. At the same time, Marxist revolutionists were gaining force throughout all the rural areas of Colombia, sponsoring themselves with money from the drug industry and kidnappings. Russell decided the best way to help the needy people in this area was to start a fishing business and give country people an alternative way of making a living that was not related to cocaine production. He would offer jobs for over 200 fishermen and use his airplane to fly the fish from the rural jungle rivers to the market places in the local towns.

One of the most terrifying and life-changing experiences Russell ever had began on August 14, 1983, when he was taken captive by Marxist guerrillas. For five grueling months he was held hostage deep within the Colombian jungle. During this time he wrote his first book, an autobiography titled *Rescue the Captors*. He realized that while many were seeking and praying for his freedom, little or nothing was being done to free his captors from the bonds of war, violence, and atheism. From that point on, Russell began to pray and intercede for these men and all the men and women that were hopelessly caught in the middle of Colombia's ruthless civil conflict.

After his release on January 3, 1984, he was deeply encouraged by many to leave Colombia with his family for good. Despite all the contrary advice, Russell and his wife, Marina, remained in Colombia and for many years worked with evangelistic crusades throughout the entire country and in family-oriented radio ministry. During this time, Russell also completed his work on the Jubilee Bible, a translation purposed to revise "back" toward the Reformation (instead of "forward" into modernism) and return as close as possible to the roots of the pure message and pure language of the original Bible manuscripts.

It wasn't until many years later that the Lord finally opened the doors to evangelize the people that had been on Russell's heart since his kidnapping. After 20 years, many of the young men and women that had held him hostage and had become his friends during his captivity had become important leaders in the communist guerrilla movement. These old friendships were the link God used to open communication once again with hostile people who were controlling most of the rural, war-stricken areas. Over 800 pastors and missionaries had been run out of eastern Colombia, which by turn of the century had become a spiritual void, when the Lord opened the doors for a Christian radio station to transmit out from this area.

Russell began a full-fledged peace campaign focused toward these conflict areas, encouraging the fighting men and women that the only way to have real peace in Colombia was if each of them had a clean conscience before God and each other. A peace reformation that was focused on individuals, changing one heart at a time for the Lord. Soon many more radio stations were on the air with healthy, soul-inspiring Colombian music to lure in the difficult audience and short gospel messages that would surprise them before they could change the dial. As more and more individuals began to turn to the Lord, the stations altered their programming and before long, entire sermons were being requested over the frequencies.

With more and more guerrillas, paramilitary, and soldiers listening to the radio stations, Russell began to visit these violent areas that had been neglected for years by mission organizations. With logistical help from VOM and Galcom He began to travel and distribute Christian literature, Bibles and solar-powered radios locked on to the Christian radio frequencies. He has spent many years penetrating these hostile places, protected by God despite the great risks.

Then, just a few years ago, God answered another one of his prayers. The Lord provided him with another airplane similar to the one he flew before his captivity. Today, Russell works full time in the peace campaign and flies over the Colombian jungle launching what he calls Truth Packs from his little airplane. These Truth Packs consist of Christian literature, a Bible and a solar-powered Galcom radio tied to a parachute. Russell flies over coca fields, drug labs, guerrilla and paramilitary camps and towns deep within the Colombian jungle that are inaccessible by conventional methods launching the Truth Packs. His second book, *The Beatitudes: God's Plan for Battle*, has made a great impact on men and women from all the fighting factions.

In this new book, *Rescue the Captors II*, Russell tells the story of how God has touched the lives of some of the men and women who held him hostage 24 years ago. Converted guerrillas are now being used by God to replace some of the missionaries and pastors who have been forced out of eastern Colombia over the past several decades due to all the violence. God is truly doing something remarkable in an area most people had long considered a lost cause.

Lisa Stendal–Hernandez
November, 2007

TO FORGIVE AND FORGET

PART I

PART I

Marina and I with Lisa (Age 3)

Spring, 1986

I stepped off the airplane onto the jet way with mixed emotions. It was good to be back in Colombia. A long time friend greeted me with a bear hug. Out of the corner of my eye I noticed two members of the secret police in civilian clothing at the top of the ramp. I was informed that these were my new body guards provided by the government for the duration of my stay in the country. Their impeccable executive brief cases really contained Uzi submachine guns. As my wife and I were being whisked through immigration and customs along with our three year old daughter, Lisa, doubts and fears began to hammer at the pit of my stomach.

I began to vividly recall the circumstances under which I had left Colombia two years before. There had been threats from Marxist guerrillas linked to politics and even the Mafia. I had been placed on a hit list. My strong Christian convictions had made several of my enemies uncomfortable. They had made me a target. Some long time acquaintances, apparently for no other reason than good old-fashioned respect, had intervened on my behalf. My name was removed from the list of those to be killed and graciously transferred over to the list of those to be kidnapped.

The account of the five month ordeal that followed *(Rescue the Captors)* I wrote during the time I was held hostage by FARC rebels. It was published six months after my release on January 3, 1984. This book had helped open many doors for ministry and speaking engagements throughout the USA and Canada. It had even been recommended or required reading for certain government officials in the Reagan White House and in the State Department.

A Colombian industrialist from Medellin named Alberto del Corral had translated the book into Spanish and financed the first edition of 10,000 copies. I was in Minnesota when I received Alberto's call from Colombia asking if I could return for a couple of weeks and help launch the Spanish edition of the book. He had even sent me a round trip ticket.

This magnanimous gesture, however, had caused a bit of trouble be-

Jungle Pilot

tween me and my wife. Marina had graciously put up with the intense travel schedule of the past two years as we had crisscrossed North America speaking in churches, schools, universities, and other facilities on an average of several times per day. To my knowledge we never spent more than two weeks in the same town, living out of suitcases. We had no credit cards and no fixed monthly income.

Marina, who at the time did not speak fluent English, had left her home, country, friends and family to remain at my side. Now, she wanted to return to Colombia with me. I objected on the grounds that it was much too dangerous. She and our daughter, Lisa, had also been the objectives of numerous and ongoing threats. A widow of means in Minneapolis, Juanita Whitby, had graciously provided us with the use of a small apartment in her home. I felt that Marina and Lisa should wait for me in Minneapolis.

This was very difficult for Marina to accept. However, when she finally said yes, I hesitated. What if God really wanted us to return to Colombia as a family? Marina and I asked God to show us what to do. I asked God to provide the airfare for Marina and Lisa to accompany me to Colombia if this were indeed His will. Since there were a number of churches and Christian individuals who had expressed interest in helping us should we decide to return to Colombia, I asked God to provide the airfare from an unusual, different source. If God were to send us the airfare and expenses from a source that was not a church and that had nothing to do with Christian missions, I would feel confident.

Marina and I in San Martin 1986

A couple days later we received a check for two thousand dollars from the chairman of the Minnesota Republican Party. He said that he had heard that I was going to travel to Colombia and that he would like to provide the airfare and expenses so that my wife and daughter could accompany me. He told me that he was aware of all the ad honorem speaking engagements that I was doing in the Twin Cities public schools against drug abuse and that this was a small token of his appreciation. So it had been decided. Marina, Lisa and I would return as a family.

Now, back in Colombia, my new secret police body guards were giving me security briefings. We were to travel in several vehicles. There were "red zones". Going out after dark was not advisable. This all began to conflict with what I perceived as the clear leading of the Lord. I needed to be able to accept speaking engagements anywhere, anytime. Just the thought of arriving at a small church in a poor neighborhood in two large cars filled with machine-gun toting police was more than I could bear. A few days later, I went to see the general. I thanked him for providing such excellent security and told him I was returning his men. I felt like David when he tried to put on Saul's armor.

The General smiled and told me that he understood. However, since the US Embassy had requested that security be provided for me, he felt that I should go over and see them too.

Over at the Bogotá US Embassy, they were aghast at the idea of me running around Colombia with no body guards and no security briefings. One US official down at the NAS even offered to lend me his gun! I admitted that in the past I had always carried a weapon, but now, I felt that God would protect me wherever He wanted me to go. My heart told me that it would not be prudent to tell the good folks down at the embassy some of the things I was planning to do next.

Pastor in front of a
closed church building

Marina and I journeyed to Medellin to meet with Alberto del Corral and to launch the book. Doors were opening everywhere. We went to see a respected Roman Catholic priest named Rafael Garcia-Herreros, who had gone on national television to ask the guerrillas to release me while I had been kidnapped. He had also rallied people all over the country to pray for me. He had a national television program and a new FM radio station located in Bogotá. Garcia-Herreros told me he was starting what he called a National Crusade for Reconciliation. He wanted two men to lead it: one Roman Catholic and one Protestant. I was asked to be the Protestant co-director.

When I wanted to know what this would involve Garcia-Herreros had said, "I don't have any money to pay you. You will have to raise your own support, but I really need you. I read your book and this is the message we need. Colombia is supposed to be over 95% Roman Catholic but the vast majority of the people are not born again. Colombia needs to be re-evangelized. The people need to be touched by the Holy Spirit. I will give you primetime evening and morning on my radio station. You can use my name to open doors for evangelism in schools, universities, police stations, army bases and in parishes across the nation. I want to help you reach every segment of Colombian society."

Marina and I thanked Garcia-Herreros for his outstanding offer. We were scheduled to return to Minneapolis in just a few days and we had no financial provision to remain in Colombia. Even if we were to attempt to raise money in the US how many of our Protestant friends would contribute if they knew we would be working for a Roman Catholic priest!

For some time, I had been formulating a plan of action. My father was voicing repeated concern and urgency regarding my brother, Chaddy, who we had not heard from in close to two years. Shortly after my release from the kidnapping, Chaddy had convinced me to fly him back out to the jungle. With much reluctance, I had flown him back out to our ranch at Chaparral. This area was now deep in guerrilla-held territory and almost no news filtered in or out. Rumor had it that Chaddy was still out there on the farm, but there had been no direct contact or message for all this time.

I had abandoned a large cold storage facility, ice plant, generator, and rice mill at Chaparral when I left Colombia in the spring of 1984 after being released by the guerrillas. Now, my mental plan-

The Red Toyota

ning went into high gear, "Holy week is coming up. What if I get in our old red Toyota jeep and drive out to Chaparral on Good Thursday? I can make contact with Chaddy and maybe retrieve some of my abandoned equipment. If so, this may provide the finances for me to take advantage of this astounding offer from Rafael Garcia-Herreros."

Amazingly, the two people who should have been counted on to veto such a plan both approved. My dad was deeply concerned for Chaddy and my wife desperately wanted us to be able to remain in Colombia with her friends and family.

I quickly recruited two friends to accompany me, Ramiro and Armando. We left Marina and Lisa in San Martin and took off that afternoon for the 16 hour drive through guerrilla territory to Chaparral. After dark when we were an hour or so past Puerto Lleras, the voltage regulator burned out and the generator quit charging the battery. I quickly disconnected the tail lights, the running lights and the dash lights leaving only the low beam headlights to conserve the limited power of the battery. Even so, I soon realized that the battery would not be sufficient to run the vehicle all night and permit us to arrive at our destination.

We pulled over and rigged an emergency light so that Ramiro could take a look at the voltage regulator. There were several spools of thin copper wire, and he proceeded to unwind them all until he found a burnt wire; then he patched it, wound back up all the wires, we started the jeep, and it worked!

In the mean time, we were overtaken by a large convoy of gasoline car-tankers headed for the drug fields. Amazingly, they all had no tail lights, no running lights, only low beam headlights. I found out later that this was to help conceal them from government aircraft and to identify them to the guerrillas who were under orders to let them pass unmolested. We managed to pull out as the last vehicle in the convoy, and due to the bizarre circumstances, our vehicle now had the exact same appearance as the rest.

We arrived at a neighbor's farm at 4 A.M. Rafael Parra, better known as Rafico, had been a good friend for many years. Normally an early riser he had decided to sleep in one day out of the year, Good Friday. Not so. We got him out of bed and down the line with us to Chaparral in his eight ton Ford truck.

At Chaparral, we picked up Chaddy with our Ford 5000 tractor. When I explained

Armando and Chaddy

about rescuing my abandoned equipment, Chaddy said, "We better hurry, the guerrillas have been talking about taking the generator to power one of their new towns. They are just waiting for the river to rise enough for them to load it onto a boat. This year is the longest dry season I can remember, and the swamp is still dry enough for us to get through to the fish house in Rafico's truck."

We drove through the swamp and made it to the fish house by a little after 6 A.M. Chaddy hooked the hydraulics of the tractor onto the heavy generator and cold storage equipment and quickly loaded it piece by piece into the large truck. Low, threatening clouds were on the horizon, and rain drops were starting to fall as we feverishly drove back through the swamp.

Back at the ranch house, Chaddy began to fill me in on the past two years. We had to break it short, however, because the rain intensified and we had several more swamps to drive through before we could get back to the main road. Chaddy said, "I have been making friends with some of the guerrillas, and one of their top commanders has been asking questions about God. If I can line up a meeting, will you come back and talk with him?"

I told Chaddy to clear up the airstrip and that I would attempt to put dad's old Cessna 170 into flying condition so that I could come back out and see him.

We made it back through all the swamps as the rain poured down. Now, we had to go back over the dangerous main road in broad daylight.

The hours went by; we passed through crossing after crossing. No one stopped us. It was Good Friday! Finally we went through a

Here I am with
Rafico and family

crossing and saw the guerrillas sitting at a *cantina* with their motorcycles parked outside. As we continued down the road, Armando and Ramiro kept looking out the back window to see if anyone was following us. The Ford truck with our equipment was in front of us, and Rafico was really stepping on the gas.

Armando and I had been witnessing to Ramiro who was not a Christian. Somehow our conversation got onto the subject of peace or "shalom", in Hebrew, and I explained to Ramiro that as a Christian we can have peace inside even in the midst of very difficult circumstances. True peace is when God provides everything that we need and is linked to the number seven in Scripture. Several hours later we stopped in Puerto Lleras, the first town we considered semi-safe to get something to drink. When we got back in the jeep, Ramiro noticed the odometer. It said 77,777.7!

CHAPTER 3

We unloaded the equipment at my father's house in San Martin. I hired another non-Christian mechanic, who, along with Ramiro, helped me clean up and paint the equipment so that we could attempt to sell it. Marina cooked for all of us as we worked on the equipment and on the old Cessna 170 at the San Martin airport.

One day we were invited to a funeral and who should I run into but Roberto? Roberto, a mentally retarded boy was known as the town fool. Yet he always had a big smile on his face as he helped people bring their groceries home from the market in a large two wheel cart that my parents had bought for him. Somehow, Roberto had managed to support his mother and sisters for many years. In spite of his limited mental capacity, I have never heard him complain. He was forever grateful and overflowing with thanks for the 100 dollar hand cart that my parents had bought for him years ago.

When I saw Roberto, however, it was as though someone had stuck a hot knife into me. I instantly remembered a promise that I had made to God while I was being held hostage out in the guerrilla camp two and a half years before. I had been musing about the past and thinking about what I could have done differently. Roberto had come to mind and I told God that if I ever got another opportunity that I would like to do more for him. In fact, I promised God that if I ever saw him again that I would give him all the money that I had in my pockets.

Now, here was Roberto, right in front of me and I had all of our meager finances "safe" in my pocket for lack of an adequate place back at the house. Well, I balked. God could never expect me to fulfill a promise like that under circumstances like this. Yet, as I left the funeral, my heart smote me and I said to the Lord, "If you really want me to give him all the money (leaving us completely stranded) let me run into him again."

I thought I had just left Roberto back at the funeral when here he was again, standing ahead of me at the next corner I had to pass on my way home. Roberto came forward to greet me beaming and thanking me for the

Flying with my dad

thousandth time for the help that our family had given him years before. With a lump in my throat I reached into my pocket and placed all my money into his hand. "I know you can't count this," I told him, "but please take it home to your mother, and she will help you."

As I saw Roberto happily head home, I knew deep inside that I had done the right thing. When I got home, however, I ran straight into trouble. Marina was waiting for me at the door. She was not feeling well, and she wanted to return immediately to Bogotá. She was tired of cooking for my uncouth mechanics. Furthermore, she was against the idea of spending money fixing up all this old rusty equipment. I told her I would try to borrow some money in the morning and send her in to Bogotá.

"What do you mean, 'borrow' money," she asked, "Where is our money? I want to go to Bogotá now!"

So, I had to tell her about Roberto and my promise to God. When she heard the story she told me that I was the town fool!

By morning Marina had decided to stick it out and stay with me in San Martin. We had no sooner finished cleaning and painting the equipment when someone drove up to the front door and purchased everything. He paid us with twelve checks, one for each month of the year. Now we had the support to work with Rafael Garcia-Herreros for an entire year! Marina's "illness" turned out to be nothing serious. It was just morning sickness. She was a couple months pregnant with Alethia, our second girl, born Oct. 1, 1986.

Rescue
The
Captors II

CHAPTER 4

May, 1986

Chaddy sent word that he had lined up the meeting with the guerrilla leader and that the airstrip was ready. The old Cessna 170 was almost airworthy and the local police chief gave me permission to take off even though some paper work was pending. An hour and a half later, I landed at Chaparral and Chaddy was delighted.

A group of armed guerrillas came out of the woods and quickly surrounded the airplane. I recognized Javier as the leader. He walked over and said, "What are you doing here? We thought you would leave and never come back."

The main leader, named John 40, was nowhere to be found. Chaddy suggested that we get in the plane and fly over the guerrilla camp to let him know that I had arrived. A couple minutes after take off I spotted a fast speedboat going up river. Chaddy said, "Buzz that boat, It's him!"

As we approached the boat it began to swerve

frantically from side to side and finally disappeared into a clump of sword grass on the edge of the jungle. Chaddy said, "Don't make another pass. They don't look very happy. Maybe they will start shooting at us."

A couple hours later they showed up at our place and invited us to a soccer match down river. Chaddy and I got in the boat and away we went. There were guerrillas everywhere. The soccer match was between two rural neighborhoods with guerrillas playing on both teams. They left their weapons and cartridge belts in a big pile to one side of the field. At the end of the day, the commander asked Chaddy to accompany him in his speed boat and left me to return to Chaparral in a huge dugout canoe powered by a large outboard motor along with many of the local people. Two guerrillas climbed in the prow as we shoved off.

Everything seemed fine until we made a stop about half way to our Chaparral fish house. Two members of the communist syndicate committee called the guerrillas and the motor man up to the top of the bank for a long consultation with occasional wild gestures in my direction. I recognized one of the men as Luis Capera. He was my only remaining enemy in the area. On several occasions he had broken into our business to steal things, including an outboard motor. It began to look like he was trying to find a way to get rid of me before I had a chance to have a good talk with the top guerrilla commander. For what seemed like an eternity, I waited, wondering what to do.

Then, all-of-a-sudden the wife of the motor man

went into action. She started the outboard motor and began revving it up wildly. Startled, the motor man stuck his head over the bank to see what was going on with his prized possession.

She yelled up the bank in a commanding tone, "We are leaving now!"

Luis Capera stuck his head over the bank and snarled, "Who says?"

She yelled back, "Martín says," and nodded at me. (In Colombia I go by my middle name, Martin)

My heart sank. But the motor man and the two guerrillas trotted meekly down the bank and into the boat leaving Luis Capera up there talking to himself as we pulled away. I breathed a loud sigh of relief.

Soon we were back at the Chaparral fish house where Chaddy had left the tractor. It had huge, oversize rice tires and no fenders. I started it up and the two guerrillas climbed on behind. When we hit the swamp on the way back to the main ranch house I really opened her up. Mud went flying everywhere, and when we got there the guerrillas looked like tar babies. They

Some Guayabero Indians with a 200 lb. catfish.
My sister, Gloria, in background

looked so strange that it was all I could do to keep Chaddy's Rotweiler, Killer, from tearing into them. Soon, all the men disap-

Indians near Caño Jabón

peared leaving us alone with John 40, commander of the 16th front of the FARC.

We talked for most of the night as I did my best to answer his questions regarding God, creation, the universe, and life in general. He seemed particularly amazed that I would come out and see him after what had happened to me at the hands of his comrades. I told him that I would always, to the best of my ability, make myself available to talk about spiritual matters but that the best way to resolve doubts and questions is to ask God Himself. God delights in having direct contact with each and every one of us.

John formed his men in the morning in our back yard and we issued them Bibles or New Testaments. Chaddy had several cases of them stashed under his bed. The guerrillas were given orders to read the Bible.

Later in the morning, I pulled the airplane out from under some trees where we had hidden it from the sight of any over-flying aircraft and put on an air show for the guerrillas. One of them even insisted on going with me, rifle and all. He was greeted as a hero upon our return and became an instant friend. The same was true of the two guerrillas who had been in the boat and on the tractor with me the night before.

John 40 gave me a bear hug when we said goodbye. He told me that I had given him quite a scare when we buzzed his speedboat the day before. He had thought that we were the government, so he zigzagged into the sword grass at the edge of the river and took off running into a clump of sword grass and stickers. He had apparently run the boat right out of the water, and he still had a few cuts and scrapes. I knew that a lasting impression had been made which would prove to be the beginning of a long term friendship.

Guajibo Indian friends near Guaviare River

CHAPTER 5

*W*When I got back to San Martin from this second trip my mother was there, eager for news of Chaddy. I ended up flying her back out to Chaparral along with Marina and Lisa. Mom said she would have to see for herself if Chaddy was really evangelizing the guerrillas according to my report. This time we spent a couple weeks.

The guerrillas were in the midst of forming a political party called *La Unión Patriótica*, or UP (The Patriotic Union). They were planning political rallies in all the remote areas under their control. They sent word to Chaddy about a rally to be held up *Caño Danta* (Tapir Creek) across the river from us. They wanted to borrow our generator to power their sound system.

Chaddy said yes, but on one condition. He told the communist organizers that his mother was visiting and that she had a movie projector along with some films about the life of Jesus Christ. If Mom could show her movies to the people they would be welcome to use our generator for their political rally.

Not only was the deal accepted but Chaddy killed a steer and took the meat out to the site of the rally in the early morning. He sent a boat back for us later in the day. When we got there everyone was happily eating some of Chaddy's roast beef. He then began to set up the movie projector with a large white sheet as the screen.

Communist political organizers and guerrillas began to trickle in. Chaddy turned on the movie projector, and everyone began to watch the Gospel film. About fifteen minutes into the movie there was a commotion. One of the visiting political leaders of the UP began to have a fit.

"This is religious propaganda," he yelled, "and we can't have it."

Chaddy replied, "No, this is history; watch it and you might learn something."

By now, Chaddy had managed to slip his strong arm around the irate leader's shoulders turning him back towards the film and face to face with a good part of the crowd who had been following him out.

Finally, in desperation, the communist political leader shouted, "By God, I'm an atheist!"

It brought down the house. Everyone, including the guerrillas howled. In the meeting, the top political UP leader for the entire area, a man named Jericho, had quietly slipped up along side of Chaddy who quickly put his other arm around him.

In a loud, penetrating voice Chaddy announced

to the laughter-stricken crowd, "We are not like him," with one arm still around the shoulders of the would-be atheist, "we all believe in Jesus Christ, don't we?"

Jericho spoke up and said, "Yes, Chaddy, we all believe in Jesus Christ."

The crowd turned around and everyone resumed watching the movie intently. Chaddy took Jericho and some of the other leaders over to see mom, who was running the projector. After giving Mom a glowing introduction, he told them that there was something much more important that they needed to know.

"Right now," Chaddy said, "my mother is going to tell you how to have eternal life." Then he elbowed Mom and said, "Tell em, Mom, tell em."

For the first time in my life I saw my mother at a loss for words. She was not sure what to say to all those revolutionary leaders. The movie had just come to the part where Nicodemus came by night to see Jesus. Jesus was telling him that he must be born again.

Finally Mom said to the expectant leaders, "Just watch the film, and I think you will understand."

After the film some of the political leaders tried to hook up their sound system planning to shout political anti-American slogans. Somehow no one seemed to be able to find the right cords and adapters. When the political rally began to fizzle for lack of the sound system Chaddy called Jericho off to one side and whispered in his ear.

Soon Jericho strode forward into the midst of the meeting and made an announcement with a big smile on his face, "It has been brought to my attention," he beamed, "that it

River boats at a guerrilla town

is Chaddy's mother's birthday today. We wish to honor her for her mission work with poor children, with the Indians and among all the people of the area. We are now going to suspend the political activities until a future date and turn this gathering into a special birthday party for *Señora Patricia*."

This news was met with whoops of approval from almost everyone. They had Mom get her movie projector back out and show all the rest of her films. Someone showed up with a darling pet squirrel and give it to Mom as a birthday present. In the midst of the festivities, which lasted past midnight, Chaddy fell asleep on the prow of one of the boats; he had been up since well before dawn preparing the meat.

About 10 PM there was another commotion. Chaddy had rolled over in his sleep and had fallen into the swift current of *Caño Danta*. Three or four guerrillas all spontaneously jumped into the water to fish him out!

Soon the guerrillas hung hammocks and mosquito nets and put us all to bed. Truly Mom had a birthday party to remember as well as the answer to her questions regarding Chaddy's activities over the past couple years.

I left the meeting privy to some inside information that no one else seemed aware of. First, Jericho and Chaddy had grown up together in Puerto Lleras. Jericho had been given a scholarship to study in the Soviet Union, returning to Colombia years later in an important role with the UP. Second, Luis Capera, when he saw how well we were in with the leaders had called me to one side in the middle of the birthday party.

"Regarding the past," he said, "please don't mention any of the things that I stole from you. I promise to make it right with your brother. I will pay back every cent. If the guerrilla leadership finds out they might strip me of my rank or even kill me," he pleaded.

I put my left hand on his shoulder and held out my right hand, which he shook warmly.

"I wouldn't even think of mentioning it," I told him.

Time would prove that this was the beginning of yet another critical friendship.

Proverbs 16:7

"When a man's ways please the LORD, he makes even his enemies to be at peace with him".

A MUCH MORE POWERFULL WEAPON

PART II

PART II

With Rafael Garcia-Herreros

CHAPTER 6

The years went by and Colombia continued to degenerate into more and more violence. Many if not most of the UP politicians like Jericho were gunned down in retaliation for perceived excesses committed previously by the FARC. The cocaine trade continued to prosper, fueled by the insatiable appetite of consumers in Europe and North America. Colombia soon became a major producer of heroin.

In 1987 I worked together with renowned Christian film producer, Bruce Lood, to make a one hour documentary film entitled *Cocaine: The Source and the Consequences*. Even though the film was aired in a number of major cities and even played on closed circuit TV at the White House, I could see that the message did not really sink in.

I went on tour and showed my documentary film at over one hundred schools and universities across North America. In the end it became quite clear that the vast majority of North Americans, including most of those in responsible government positions or in the news media simply refused to believe that out of control drug consumption in Europe and in the United States could ever destabilize South America or cause lasting strategic damage to the very foundations of American freedoms. I felt like a voice crying out in the wilderness.

June, 1989

Frustrated with the hedonist indifference of many North Americans, I returned to Colombia and began to speak on the radio station of my friend, Rafael Garcia-Herreros. Soon our program had one of the highest listener ratings in Bogotá.

Chaddy heard that I was back and invited me on a trip to *Caño Jabón*. This was the place where the guerrillas had kidnapped me almost six years before. Chaddy said that the guerrillas had something important that they wanted to say to me. Hundreds, if not thousands, of copies of *Rescue The Captors* had by now been distributed in guerrilla areas. With reservations and some mixed feelings I decided to go with Chaddy. What if the guerrilla leaders were upset with some of the strong statements in my book?

Chaddy and I landed in *Caño Jabón* on a Monday morning. No one had seen fit to tell us that

Giving out Bibles and Rescue The Captors

there had been a massively tragic guerrilla attack on the *Caño Jabón* police station the night before. When we arrived, the entire town was in a shambles. A couple hundred guerrillas had attacked the police station about midnight unaware that some of the policemen were outside the station sleeping in town. These men snuck up behind the guerrillas and killed or wounded several dozen of them. The streets were filled with blood stains and even occasional body parts. Government helicopters were still pursuing the guerrillas who had fled in boats down the river.

And who should we run into but Carlos R. and Luis Capera? Carlos was the man who had betrayed me and set up the events leading up to my kidnapping years before. Back then he had owned the most prosperous general store in town. Now, he was reduced to a small fruit stand in the middle of the street. On a previous occasion, I had given him a hug and reassured him that I held no hard feelings. He, in turn had helped me distribute New Testaments and copies of *Rescue The Captors* all over town.

Both Carlos and Luis confided that they had both spent most of the night on their knees crying out to God to spare them, their families and their meager possessions. We explained to Luis and Carlos that we had come to evangelize the guerrillas and that we needed a boat and motor. A few minutes later they located a dark, handsome man with a mustache and a large gold chain around his neck who was also a friend of Chaddy.

The man with the mustache owned several businesses and also had a beautiful speed boat. When he found out that I wanted to evangelize the guerrillas, he fueled up his prized boat and offered it to us free of charge.

Chaddy left me at our fish house at Chaparral and then took off down river after the guerrillas. To my complete consternation, he showed up a few hours later with the two main guerrilla commanders, John 40 of the 16th front and Giovanni, now commander of the 7th front who had kidnapped me in 1983. I had not seen Giovanni since my release. He strode over with a big smile and gave me a hug. His second in command, Noel, seemed to blend into the background, observing everything.

Meeting with Noel

Noel had also been present during my captivity.

I was amazed that right after losing so many men and in the midst of intense government pursuit that they would drop everything and return to speak with me. Guerrillas are known for their audacity and for doing the unexpected. This was certainly a case in point. Later, I learned that Giovanni's wife had been seriously injured in that failed attack the night before.

John and Giovanni took Chaddy and me off to

one side and carefully told us of the purpose of their visit. "We have been commissioned on behalf of the entire FARC guerrilla movement," they said, "to apologize and ask for forgiveness. Everyone recognizes that it was a big mistake for us to have kidnapped you."

Without missing a beat, Chaddy replied, "If you are genuinely repentant then that means you should give back the ransom money that you took from us."

"We are not authorized to do that," they replied, "but we can take it up with the top leadership."

"For my part," I said, "tell them that I have no hard feelings. What some may have meant for evil, God has used for great good. Tell your leaders that if they will return the 55 thousand dollars that was paid as a ransom we will use it to help build a hospital in Caño Jabón. From the looks of last night, that town really needs one!"

These people have just recieved
Rescue The Captors in an area torn
apart by violence

December, 1991

The radio ministry in Bogota continued. By now, I had lost track of the number of printings of *Rescue The Captors* in both English and Spanish that had been distributed mostly by free will offerings all over North and South America. Many thousands of copies had now been given away in guerrilla areas. Many people all over had responded to the Gospel message of the book by giving their hearts to the Lord.

One night after I finished speaking at a church in Bogota, a man came up to me and thanked me profusely for writing the book. I was deep in the jungle out behind Calamar," he said, "and when I read your book, I immediately gave my heart to the Lord." "How did you get the book?," I asked, "I don't remember distributing any in the Calamar area."

"Oh, it was easy," he said, "the guerrillas came by and one of them sold me your book!"

About the same time, Chaddy was contacted by Giovanni and asked to travel to a remote river crossing. Chaddy went, thinking it would be just a normal meeting. To his surprise he was put on a horse and taken three days ride deep into the jungle. Giovanni's wife was on another horse with a small baby. In the midst of the journey a rotten bridge gave way under her horse and the helpless baby fell into the turbulent waters. Chaddy dove in and saved the baby in the nick of time.

It turned out that Chaddy had been invited to a meeting of front commanders of the entire eastern block of the FARC. For the next week, Chaddy was given the honor of sleeping in the next bed over from Jorge Briceno, known as the *Mono Jojoy*, now the military commander of the entire guerrilla movement.

Giovanni introduced Chaddy to all the guerrilla commanders, and he was given an hour to speak. The purpose of the invitation was to present our request for the return of the ransom money. Chaddy, who had never been much of a public speaker, rose to the occasion. He shared his own testimony of all that God had done in his life. Then, he told them that repentance and forgiveness are incomplete when we do not do our best to make restitution when we know that we have done something wrong.

Chaddy told them of my offer to use the ransom money to help build a hospital in Caño Jabon, which would be useful to everyone.

At the end of his presentation, a vote was taken. Under the circumstances I thought that it was amazing that 40 per cent of the commanders voted to return the money. Among the 60 per cent that said no, many were sympathetic to us but felt that the return of the money would set a dangerous precedent for their organization.

After this, the *Mono Jojoy* got up and told Chaddy that we were wasting our time with our missionary work. He invited us to join the FARC if we really wanted to accomplish something. "Come with us," the *Mono* told Chaddy, "and I will make you the commander of an entire front!"

Chaddy politely declined the *Mono's* generous offer and exited the meeting. The *Mono*, however, continued to give Chaddy special treatment for the rest of the week until the guerrilla commander's summit was over. Chaddy was even allowed to view the secret video collection of all the guerrilla armed operations. Many of the videos ended tragically with dozens of guerrillas killed or hopelessly wounded. Somehow, behind the impeccable veneer of revolutionary discipline, many of those leaders seemed to be subliminally crying out for help.

Massive distribution of
Bibles and literature

CHAPTER 8

Over the previous 10 years, the government had participated in several peace initiatives towards the guerrillas. On several occasions they had flown my friend, Rafael Garcia-Herreros to a place called *Casa Verde* to participate in talks with Manuel Marulanda Velez, also known as, *Tirofijo,* (or Sureshot) supreme commander and founding father of the FARC. Rafael Garcia-Herreros had authorized me to make contact with regional guerrilla leaders as co-director of his National Crusade for Reconciliation. He was even able to call the President of Colombia and get government approval for my brother and me to meet with and evangelize guerrillas.

Garcia-Herreros and I were also involved on the fringes of the successful peace negotiations and demobilization of the M-19 guerrilla movement. In a parallel scenario, emerald magnate, Victor Carranza had flown us on several occasions out to help mediate the war between the heirs of Gilberto Molina and those associated with Rodriguez Gacha, better known as *El Mejicano*, (The Mexican). We had preached on occasion to crowds of more than 20,000 people at a time. In the end, the opposing factions flew in to a meeting and signed an agreement in front of us know later as the *La Paz de Quipama* (The Peace of Quipama) which lasted for many years.

Little did I know at the time, but those meetings in Quipama served to forge crucial friendships and trust with key individuals who would soon emerge as regional leaders of the paramilitary movement which, even then, was in a fledgling state.

Now, Garcia-Herreros was reaching out to the Medellin Drug Cartel. I was asked to accompany him on several trips filled with cloak and dagger intrigue as my friend negotiated the surrender of Pablo Escobar to the Colombian government.

On one occasion, we spent three days in the home of Fabio Ochoa Sr. known to some as the "God-father" of Medellin. Fabio had a strong, almost irrational hatred for Americans, but he seemed to put up with me and was even magnanimous at times. During my stay in his home with Rafael Garcia-Herreros his wife, Margot, made it clear that she had committed her life to the Lord. A few months later she divorced Fabio.

Pablo Escobar had several doubles and at times it was extremely difficult to even know for sure who we were dealing with. In the end, I am not one hundred per cent certain that the real Pablo Escobar went to jail. However, the cartel-related violence in Medellin and elsewhere tapered off and Garcia-Herreros was hailed as a hero.

A few months later, when "Pablo" escaped from prison and was killed, the health of Garcia-Herreros began to deteriorate rapidly. He passed away in the fall of 1992.

Here I am entering
a guerrilla controlled area

Chapter 9

April, 1992

Chaddy and I embarked on a journey down the Ari Ari River starting at Puerto Rico, Meta. My niece, Hepzy, who was almost four, was with us. Somehow, Hepzy, who was a very active child, had dislocated her thumb. Chaddy and I managed to put it back in position but her little hand was black and blue and quite swollen.

In a small hamlet, several hours down river, the people were quite aloof and cautious with us when we stopped for something to drink. A few minutes later some guerrillas arrived and told us to come with them. We got in the boat and after about ten minutes we pulled over next to a banana patch which was full of guerrillas. Giovanni strode down the bank with a big smile on his face and greeted us with bear hugs.

On our way down river Chaddy had been telling me about a recent river battle led by Giovanni against a naval task force that had attempted to sail up the river. The main gunboat had been sunk by the guerrillas along with six supporting vessels. Over one hundred naval infantry (marines) and crew had been killed with dozens more wounded. At that time I was told that it went down as the worst defeat of the Colombian Navy in history. Giovanni was known by his enemies as a ruthless opponent whose trademark was expert use of over-whelming force.

Giovanni, however, took one look at my little four-year-old niece, Hepzy, and melted. He insisted on hanging up his own hammock and mosquito net for her. Then, he ordered special food to be pre-pared. When he saw her bruised hand, the guer-rilla medic was immediately summoned. It wasn't until well over an hour later, after Hepzy's hand was bandaged, after she had eaten at the hand of Giovanni, himself, and after she was fast asleep in his own personal hammock that Giovanni shared the real reason he had stopped us.

After watching recent events over the past sev-eral years in the former Soviet Union and in East-ern Europe, Giovanni and many others had come to the conclusion that something was wrong with their Marxist ideology. They were searching for an-swers. Giovanni sat me down with what he called his *Estado Mayor*. They were the top men from sev-eral fronts. One of them, Noel, began to ask me questions. I soon saw that these men were deter-mined to continue with the revolution. Their rifles and the blood of comrades lost in combat were sa-cred to them. I also detected undying loyalty to their leaders.

I tried to explain to them that one false premise or false assumption at the beginning of a long chain of seemingly flawless logic could compromise the whole thing. The false premise at the very foundation of Marxism is that God does not exist. For me, I told them, God is the personification of truth and of justice. Without Him we would all be in the dark. Noel and the others pressed me for practical applications of what I was saying. They told me that they were open to any constructive criticism that I could offer.

Deciding to start with a small and apparently trivial point, I first told them that if we genuinely desire truth and justice we cannot plant lies and chaos. All of us will eventually reap what we sow. It is impossible to plant one thing and reap another. This holds true for everyone, including the US government, the Colombian government, the Roman Catholic Church, the Protestant Evangelicals and for each and every individual as well as for each guerrilla and for the entire guerrilla movement.

Then, I proceeded to relate to them my perspective regarding the practice of the guerrilla movement, which was quite prevalent at the time, to spray paint logos and revolutionary sayings on the sides of vehicles passing through guerrilla-held areas. I told them that this looked like graffiti from an inner city gang. I told them that if they were to win the respect and admiration of the people everything should be done proper and in order.

"How are you going to convince the people that you are fit to govern the nation, if you can't even do a decent job of painting your slogans," I asked?

It is interesting to note that from then on, and starting from the 7th front, the guerrillas began to carefully select their slogans, they began to make meticulous stencils and to use colors compatible with the background they were painting on. In the end, even the paramilitary and the Colombian Army began to follow their example in this.

Giovanni proudly began to show me some of the heavy weapons that he had captured. I "oohed and aahed" but then told him I had a much more powerful weapon to give him. Reaching into my bag, I produced an olive drab camouflaged Bible prepared by Armando Cifuentes, a Christian army colonel.

"This is what God says," I told Giovanni, "and if we hearken to His word everything will turn out all right in the end." Chaddy and I proceeded to issue camouflage Bibles to all of Giovanni's trusted lead-

A converted guerrilla
distributes Bibles

ers when we were interrupted by an eighty-year-old gentleman with white hair who proved to be the owner of the banana patch where we were meeting.

"Missionaries!" he cried, "I see that you are missionaries! I have been praying for over thirty years for God to send the Gospel to these boys."

The old saint came forward and held out his hand with tears in his eyes. I told the guerrilla leaders to join hands in a circle with the old man in the center. Then, I asked him to close the meeting in prayer. He knelt in the center, up against an old tomato crate and began to pray up a storm. Several of the guerrillas started to blink back tears under the powerful conviction of the Holy Spirit.

Bannana patch near the
bank of the Ari Ari River

THE LAST BIBLE TRANSLATOR

PART III

PART III

Who would have ever thought that
millions would now use the audio and internet
versions of of this Spanish Bible?

CHAPTER 10

January, 1996

For the past ten years, it had been my custom to spend the winter months traveling north in ministry across Canada and Alaska. This year was no exception. I found that in the north, unlike the lower 48 where services are primarily on Sunday morning, our ministry was welcome any day of the week and holidays were no exception. So I drove up the Alaska highway with what I felt was a tremendous message on the "Fire of God".

After years of owning old vehicles, my father and brother had purchased an almost new Oldsmobile 88, which they both claimed was the best car they had ever owned. Somehow I had managed to persuade them to lend me their pride and joy for this trip. With the addition of special snow tires, a block heater, and synthetic oil, I was confident that I now had dependable transportation.

The wonderful Oldsmobile took me to Whitehorse, where a local teenager joined me, and from there up to the Klondike near Dawson City. There I accepted an invitation to go up the Dempster Highway to Inuvik. Inuvik was in Arctic night (24 hour darkness), and from there I drove north on the ice road up the McKenzie River and over the frozen Beaufort Sea to the Inuit village of Tuktoyuktuk, the last settlement on the North American Continent.

On the way back we drove through a terrible storm and out into awesome clear sky. The sun began to peak over the horizon after we passed the Arctic Circle quite a few miles south of Inuvik. While under the storm clouds, the temperature had been a moderate 25 below. But, unknown to me at the time, the temperature had gone way, way down as the sky became clear.

As the temperature went down, the vehicle began to use much more fuel. By the time the temperature had dropped past 60 degrees below zero the fuel consumption had almost doubled. We pulled into Dempster Corner running on fumes, and as soon as we stopped at the gas pump, the power steering froze solid. In what appeared to be such nice weather we were almost oblivious to the real danger we were in. If stranded, we could have frozen to death in just a few minutes.

As I continued my trip on towards Alaska alone, I began to meditate concerning False Peace and the parallels between the present world situation and the experience that had just happened to me.

"For when they shall say, Peace and Safety; then sudden destruction shall come upon them." (1 Thessalonians 5:3).

Entering Alaska, the temperature continued to drop, and an ice fog set in. Trying to be prudent, I topped off the gas tank at every opportunity. It was dark at mid- after-

With my wife, Marina, daughters Lisa and Alethia and my son, Russell Jr. on tour in Alaska

noon as I approached Tok, Alaska, on my way to Anchorage. The temperature was 67 below. I decided to play it safe and spend the night at Fast Eddies Motel.

I shut off the Oldsmobile, plugged in the block heater, and took a shower. Then I phoned the motel receptionist and asked for a wake up call at 6 A.M. After a couple hours, I went out and checked the car, finding that even though it was plugged in, it would barely start. So all through the night, I went out and started it every hour or two. Finally, I dozed off in the motel room with the car plugged in and with the motor running. I was rudely awakened at about 4 A.M. with shouts of FIRE! FIRE! I looked outside. It was MY car that was on fire.

All our attempts to put out the fire failed. We were able to pull it clear of the eaves of the building with another vehicle just before it blew up twice. Finally the fire department arrived and sprayed down the charred remains with water that almost instantly turned to ice. I returned to my room to meditate and pray. Then I called my folks and the insurance company back in Florida where the Oldsmobile was registered, four time zones away. I had to explain twice to the girl at the State Farm Insurance Agency in Bonita Springs, Florida, where Tok, Alaska was located.

A few minutes later, I was seated at the motel restaurant with my new friends who had been in the room next to mine. After our efforts to put out the fire failed, they graciously offered to take me to Anchorage in their vehicle. As we were waiting for our breakfast to be served, the receptionist came over and asked, "Are you the gentleman from Room 17? I have been trying to give you your wakeup call."

Wake up call! I felt the voice of the Lord gently impress within my heart, *"If you will stay in the fire of my dealings, you will not need a wake up call when I come back."* Considering the present state of False Peace that has put many Christians to sleep regarding matters of extreme spiritual importance, I spent the next several days musing over the "foolish" who were awakened at midnight only to find no oil in their lamps; the "wise" who were asleep yet had oil, and who entered in to the wedding as maids of honor. (See Matthew Chapter 25). Contrast this to the Shulamite in The Song of Solomon who said,

> *"I sleep, but my heart watches for the voice of my be-loved."* (Song 5:2)

After a few more days of meetings in Alaska with some dear friends in a series of conventions I returned to Colombia from Fairbanks. State Farm Insurance lived up to their reputation. Even though the car was registered to my dad and my brother in Florida, they gave me payment for the full value of the Oldsmobile in Alaska.

I arrived back to Colombia with the insurance check in my pocket right as Wycliffe missionaries were closing their base at Lomalinda. Using the check from the Oldsmobile insurance claim as down payment, I was able to negotiate three of the houses the missionaries left behind. Little did I know at the time that this would be the site where the Lord would use us to raise up several powerful FM, AM and short wave radio stations that would reach all over eastern Colombia with echoes throughout the Spanish speaking world.

Lomalinda

FINCA BONAIRE

CHAPTER 11

It was Chaddy (6) and I (8) and Billy Townsend (9) son of Wycliffe founder, William Cameron Townsend, who were the first missionary kids to set foot on Lomalinda in the spring of 1964. We pitched our jungle hammocks between palm trees and helped my father begin construction of the missionary base which would house close to 300 missionaries dedicated to the translation of the New Testament into all the Indian languages of Colombia and Panama. Thirty-two years later, in the spring of 1996, Chaddy and I with tears in our eyes watched the last missionary airplane leave.

The kidnapping in 1994 and later death in 1995 of New Tribes missionaries Timothy Van Dyke and Stephen Welsh near Villavicencio coupled with the kidnapping of Wycliffe missionary Ray Rising in 1994 were probably some of the deciding factors which caused the large international mission agencies to pull their people out of eastern Colombia by 1996. All told, close to 800 missionaries were pulled out of eastern Colombia in the mid 90's. National pastors were also forced to leave, some of those who refused to leave were murdered and many church buildings were closed.

When the Wycliffe missionaries left Lomalinda, it was just a matter of time until the government pulled out the troops that had been guarding the missionary base. Plainclothes guerrilla militias were everywhere, and in time uniformed guerrillas in large numbers began to patrol the area. As the conflict intensified, car bombs began going off in all of the nearby towns. Roads were mined and bridges were blown up as the guerrillas advanced. Most of the 98 buildings at Lomalinda were looted by locals and two thirds of the base was destroyed in random confusion.

When my siblings and I were growing up at Lomalinda Ray Rising, a missionary radio man, was our youth leader. Ray was also from our native state of Minnesota. Now Chaddy and I, as the only missionaries remaining east of the Andes, decided that we had a certain responsibility to secure his release. Chaddy began to make trips south, across the Ari Ari River, deep into guerrilla territory, on his motorcycle. I would remain behind at the Finca Bonaire always in constant radio contact with him. Finca Bonaire was an experimental farm next to Lomalinda that Wycliffe had sold to Chaddy when they left. The guerrillas who captured Ray belonged to the 43rd front and the leader, Steven, was notorious for being anti-American and very hard to deal with.

At Finca Bonaire, I was able to reactivate a nice air-conditioned second story office where I continued work on my Bible translations. Since 1991, I had been working on a Spanish Bible which later became known as the Reina-Valera 2000. I based this work on the original translation of Casiodoro de Reina published in 1569 and compared it with the work of William Tyndale and other scholars from the Reformation as well as consulting the original Greek and Hebrew.

I wanted this translation to be very readable from the pulpit yet retain all the brilliance and depth of the original translations of the Reformation. As this Spanish Bible project progressed, I also made a copy in English on my computer. The English version was later published as the Jubilee Bible 2000. Little did I know at the time that tens of thousands of copies of this Spanish Bible in print and on solar audio players would later be distributed in guerrilla controlled areas and that this would cause an ongoing impact.[1]

The farm house at Finca Bonaire

I would be deeply engrossed in Bible study when my radio would beep. Chaddy kept finding people who had been seriously injured in the war and needed my help to alert the doctors at the nearby hospital in Puerto Lleras and coordinate

1 Millions of copies of this Bible have also been downloaded over the internet all over the Spanish speaking world.

rescue efforts so that their lives might be saved. On one of his trips across the river, Chaddy heard a rumor that something had happened to Steven and that there was a new guerrilla commander.

An untrustworthy person attempted to "guide" Chaddy out to see the top commander in a cloak and dagger situation that almost cost Chaddy his life. At the last minute everything turned around. The new guerrilla commander of the 43rd front was none other than our old acquaintance, John 40! We had not seen him for 8 years. John was delighted to see us. The multimillion dollar ransom demands for Ray Rising were dropped. Nevertheless, it continued to be a touchy situation because other commanders, including the notorious Steven, who eventually re-surfaced, all had to be convinced that they should let Ray go. After countless trips Chaddy's efforts resulted in the release of our dear friend Ray Rising in December of 1996 after 810 days in captivity.

Ray, Chaddy, Hector, Russell Jr., and I on the day of his release

CHAPTER 12

January 1998

Comparing notes with Ray Rising, he had come to the same conclusion that I had during my captivity with the guerrillas: A perfect way to reach them for the Lord in the midst of their introverted and closed society was through radio broadcasting. A few months earlier, a church in Port St. Lucie, Florida, had sent us an offering towards a radio station. Ray suggested a place in Miami that might be able to sell me some basic FM broadcasting equipment.

When I went there the manager offered me a 50 per cent discount when I told him what I wanted to use the equipment for. After summing up the cost of the transmitter, antenna and coax cable even with the discount the bill was still quite a bit more than the funds that I had available. I thanked the fellow and told him that I would come back later when I had more money. He said, "How much do you have?" I told him, and he pulled out his personal check book and covered the difference.

I got on a plane for Bogotá with the new radio transmitter. When I got home, I dug out my old stereo equipment which had a CD player and a tape deck. We found an old mixing board somewhere and rounded up tapes, CD's and records from all our friends. When I got out to Lomalinda in our 85' Suburban, the only place I could find to put the antenna was on top of an old flag pole out at Finca Bonaire. As I was trying to climb the flag pole with the antenna, a school teacher named Olivo came by on a bicycle. "Is that a radio transmitter?", he asked. When I replied in the affirmative, he asked, "Do you have a license?" I said, "Well, no, I was just going to try this thing out to see if it works." "Don't worry, I have the license!" Olivo replied.

Unbelievably, over the previous four years, no more than half a dozen special community radio station licenses had been granted in the entire nation; and the Puerto Lleras association of school teachers called Marfil (Ivory) had one. They were about to lose it and had been given an ultimatum from the government: they must be on the air in one month or lose their license. Unable to afford the necessary equipment, they were helpless; and then I showed up with the transmitter! We made a deal to put the station on the air and share the radio time.

Nevertheless, I had nagging thoughts about the Bible verse that speaks of not being unequally yoked. As the conflict around us continued to escalate, people were being killed on all sides in a dirty war where almost no one had scruples. By the time we had the radio station on the air, the school teachers all got together and signed the responsibility over to me. Apparently none of them wanted to risk getting shot over something they might say on the air!

Little by little we learned how to operate a community radio station. People would call in with messages for friends or relatives in remote places. As we put these short communications on for free, everyone in the entire area felt the need to listen just in case there might be an important message for them. We learned how to get just the right mix of Colombian typical music coupled with Gospel messages that everyone could relate to and understand. There were eight churches in town and some of them began to help us with the radio ministry.

One evening in the midst of intense fighting all around, some guerrillas showed up at the radio station with a revolutionary manifesto that they wanted to read over the air. Before they could get to the microphone someone shot down the power lines and the station went dead.

Then disaster hit. A few months later the guerrillas gave the order to close all of the evangelical churches in town. A pastor who had a program on our station was gunned down and killed. So were his two sons. All the other pastors withdrew their

A converted guerrilla
who is now an evangelist
in front of a closed church building

programs from our station, even though the guerrillas had not given the order to close it down.

On one occasion, I happened to be in the emergency room in a nearby town because Chaddy had broken his ankle while roping a cow. Just then, a pastor was brought in fatally wounded. He had been shot four times in the throat for preaching the Gospel. Only the Lord knows how many Christians have been killed in eastern Colombia over the past twenty five years for their faith in God.

With what meager funds the Lord provided we opened recording studios in Bogotá and began producing our own programs to replace the programs that had been canceled. The Lord provided just the right people. Friends would come over to our mountain side apartment on Saturday and Sunday and help me dig into the side of the mountain and load the dirt and rock onto dump trucks. The ladies would make lunch while the men worked. Then all would sit down and I would preach a message which was also recorded for the radio station.

Soon we had a nice recording studio dug right into the rock side of the mountain behind our living room wall. The Lord provided doctors, lawyers, university professors, preachers – the best of the best – as well as the recording engineers, technicians and equipment to make everything work.

I began to draw concentric circles on maps of Colombia and mail them to my friends telling them about the areas that we needed to cover with gospel radio messages in the midst of all the conflict. Many thought I was a dreamer, and maybe they were right. After lots of prayer support on all sides the Lord gave us an AM station, two short wave stations, and then more FM stations. We now have much more radio coverage than I had ever dreamed of.

Colombian country musicians started to get touched by God and then through their witness one of the top Colombian recording engineers gave his heart to the Lord. Previously an alcoholic dedicated to recording the music liked by the guerrillas and the drug growers, Henry Sanchez now began to show us and our fledgling engineers the intimate secrets of making good recordings.

Soon our Bogotá studio engineer, Fernando Alarcón, began to outdo the quality of many of the secular studios as God started to make a huge change in the content of the typical music of Colombia, Venezuela and Mexico. In more recent years Christian country musicians Rick and Bebe Svenddal began to visit us in Colombia on a yearly basis to help record music for our radio stations and to work with Colombian musicians who have been coming to the Lord.

Rick and Bebe Svenddal

CHAPTER 13

One day out at the Lomalinda radio station early in the morning a fellow came walking through the fields towards our new radio tower that the local townspeople had helped us erect. I invited him into the house and sat him down at the kitchen table just as my wife, Marina, was serving breakfast. Halfway though the meal we noticed the nine millimeter pistol in his waistband and the hand grenade in one of his front shirt pockets identifying him as guerrilla militia. We had been reminiscing old times and small talk about when he had worked for me as a fisherman many years before on the lower Guaviare River. Abruptly, he stunned us with his next comment. He said, "You know, some of us kind of like your radio programs. If the people listen to you and change their behavior then maybe we won't have to shoot them!" We sent him on his way with a bag full of *Rescue the Captors* and camouflage New Testaments to share with any of his comrades who might have similar thoughts.

Our Bogota studio that we dug out of the side of the mountain

Oddly, encouraged by this and other amazing incidents, I began to travel into the countryside to visit the people and distribute books and Bibles. I was pleasantly surprised to find that everywhere our radio signal is present, I am received with open arms by almost everyone. This encouraged me to do everything possible to increase the coverage of our station. The school teachers from Marfil began to accompany me into remote areas and help with the distribution of our literature.

Soon we had people traveling by river launch, by truck, by bus, by canoe, by motorcycle and even on horseback with boxes of books. No matter how much literature we gave away, the Lord always supplied more. And then, another miracle happened. Galcom International began to send us solar powered radios locked onto our frequencies. The distribution of these radios (which never need batteries) really began to boost our listening audience.

For more than five years pitched battles took place close to our Lomalinda radio station on an almost continual basis. Once close to five hundred guerrillas camped out at the station; then, a few days later over one thousand soldiers arrived. In some of the battles hundreds of men were killed or wounded. Sometimes car bombs that went off in Puerto Lleras, four kilometers away, scattered the body parts of innocent civilians all over town.

Despite the adverse circumstances, the ministry grew until it took eight or more people to run the radio stations. We were able to procure an additional three houses surrounding our original property. In order to get in or out of the area, sometimes we had to drive through actual battle lines on impossible roads. Military aircraft would drop parachute flares at night and shoot at guerrillas who were attacking military or police outposts nearby. Almost all the buildings for at least a ten mile ra-

Our first radio station at Finca Bonaire

dius had bullet holes in them except ours and a few others.

When the churches in our entire area were shut down (and they stayed shut down for several years) I was advised by "savvy" locals to tone down our radio broadcasts lest our radio stations suffer a similar fate. However, when we consulted with the Lord, we decided to do the opposite. With all the evangelical churches shut down and with our radio stations still operating, we began to feel that this was the time to really intensify the message.

Here I am at our Lomalinda studios

THE LAST "FIESTA" OF PUERTO TOLEDO

PART IV

PART IV

Translating the dynamic message of evangelist
Len Carter to the paramilitary in Casibare

CHAPTER 14

From late 1998 until the end of 2001 the government of Colombian President Andres Pastrana demilitarized a huge area larger than the country of Switzerland immediately to the south of our radio station at Lomalinda. This was for the purpose of peace talks with the guerrillas. In early 2002 after the so called peace process had failed, the Colombian military began to retake this zone. I knew ahead of time that any "Peace" Process that excludes the Prince of Peace is bound to fail.

A little known detail about the demilitarized zone is that it also became a haven for musicians specializing in the *Norteña* protest music of northern Mexico. This music is played with an accordion, a bass guitar, a *bajo sexto* (special Mexican 12 string guitar), and a drum set. Since the guerrilla commanders had quite a taste for this type of music, many talented musicians catered to them in the relative safety of the demilitarized zone.

When this zone came to an abrupt end, many

musicians fled to Bogotá. Months later I found some of them practically starving to death in the big city and began witnessing to them. As they began to open up to the Gospel, we took them to our studio and began to record new music in the *Norteña* style but with a different message. Then one day I got an inspiration.

What if we were to send some of our new music to the guerrilla commanders? In fact, what if we were to load up a team of musicians with the necessary sound equipment and go back into the war zone with a different Peace Campaign? Our Peace initiative would be aimed at the individual. The message would be in the typical music that they like, encouraging them to repent and to maintain a clean conscience before God and before their fellow man.

My siblings and I grew up among the Indian tribes that my parents and other missionaries wanted to reach with the Gospel. We had to learn their language and culture in order to reach them. If we had a special place for them in our hearts they would eventually perceive it and open their hearts to the Lord. We began to treat the different armed groups in a similar manner, knowing that we must seek the Lord and learn how to relate to them. After recording a cassette and a CD we assembled an impromptu "evangelistic" team and headed for Puerto Lleras.

Some of the members of our team were soundly converted. Others "thought" that they might be saved and few others were even more confused regarding their eternal future but felt that to go with us was the right thing for them to do. All of us knew that to carry out our endeavor was definitely going to risk all our lives.

One third of the town had already been destroyed in all the fighting

When we got to Puerto Lleras with our equipment, there was no one in the town hall to give us permission to use the municipal covered arena. The mayor and his entire government had fled town long before and for six months no one had even collected the garbage (the guerrillas had taken most of the municipal machinery and vehicles, including the garbage truck!). So we just went over to the arena in the town square and began setting up our equipment.

Armed guerrilla militia in plain clothes were strolling around, and other armed men belonging to their illegal yet mortal enemies, the paramilitary, were also rumored to be around the fringes of the town. People began to gather to see what was going to happen. Then a company of soldiers appeared, and the commanding officer came over and asked me who had given permission for us to have this event in such a dangerous atmosphere. I told him that I was responsible, and he looked at me for a while and then said that we could proceed as long as we shut down the meeting by 11 P.M.

Bombs had been going off all over

The live band began to sing, and the bleachers filled up. We had soldiers behind the platform, guerrilla militia at the opposite end and paramilitary in-between. Since we had lots of Gospel messages going out over the radio station, I decided not to bog this situation down with long messages. We kept the messages very short and sang all different kinds of music.

The first night our MC from Bogotá (who was clueless regarding the local political situation) tried to get a response out of the crowd who were sitting on "left" and "right" facing bleachers. He would say, "Lets hear it from the right" and all those on the right hand bleachers (which were laced with paramilitary) would cheer loudly. However, when he would say, "Now let's hear it from the left" even though the left hand bleachers were full of people our MC could not figure out why no one would say a thing!

All of a sudden, the lights went out, and I braced myself for pandemonium. I wondered if the two sides would start a shoot-out across the bleachers full of people in the dark. After breathlessly praying for a few minutes, the lights came back on.

Then, after a few hours an amazing thing began to happen. People began to come up to me on the side of the platform and tell me with tears in their eyes how much this meant to them. They told me the town was about to be shot or blown to pieces and our presence had changed things and given them hope. Some came under conviction and wanted to turn to the Lord even though we had not even given an altar call!

One man, whom I had been praying for, came up and said that he could not stand himself and asked how he could find the Lord. We continued for three nights with varied styles of typical music tailored to the situation at hand. I knew that the guerrillas had been watching and analyzing our performance. On the third night what I was hoping for happened. Word came from two guerrilla towns way across the river. They wanted to extend an invitation for us to come and sing in their towns.

Waiting for soldiers to clear
guerrilla mines from the road

CHAPTER 15

Accepting the invitation, we loaded up our team and our equipment and headed south across the river deep into guerrilla territory to the town of Villa La Paz. We were received by a long-time acquaintance named Zacarias who as part of the guerrilla movement was in charge of the peasants of the town. Zac had been one who years before in Mapiripan, near our old Chaparral ranch, had helped "move" me from the list of those to be killed onto the list of those to be kidnapped (kind of like Judah in the story of young Joseph in the book of Genesis). We started to unload our equipment in their local community center but then they had second thoughts.

There were still huge blood stains on the ground in front of the pink community center left over from a nasty shoot-out the night before. Hastily, before anyone else from our team could see the pools of blood, Zac had us move our event a couple blocks away to the largest *cantina* in town on the corner of the main street. After all, they wanted to give us a good impression of their town.

Zac took me aside and said, "Here things work like this: In order to invite you here I have to guarantee with my life that you are not a government spy. You, in turn, have to guarantee with your life each and every member of your team". By orders of the guerrillas every bar, house of ill repute, pool hall or other establishment was closed for the night. We were the only show in town.

As our band began to play and sing the *cantina* filled up with townspeople and guerrillas. Zac was so overjoyed to see me that he brought his entire family to the event. In the middle of the evening, Carlos Mario Vasquez, a famous singer who had joined us, began to sing a hit song about the guerrillas that had gone all over Colombia. The song told the story of how a desperate man had left his wife, children and family to join the guerrillas out in the mountains. It had, in fact, become like a theme song for many of them. Carlos and I had written a changed version of the song in which the guerrilla repents and finds the Lord.

Cold shivers went up and down my spine when Carlos launched into the changed version of the song in the middle of the event. What if they didn't like it? What if they got very upset with us for having changed their song? I began to pray.

The guerrillas melted. One tough commander with lots of weapons and equipment began to weep. He came over and put his arms around me and said, "Thank you, no one has ever cared about us like this before." Zac was in tears and left the meeting early. We were all given free room and board. The guerrilla leadership of Villa La Paz then sent us on to the next town, Puerto Toledo, with a wonderful recommendation to the guerrilla leadership there.

CHAPTER 16

If the guerrillas had a capital city in the area, Puerto Toledo was it. It was also a forbidden city to outsiders. We were received with royal treatment. A local hotel had been commandeered for us to sleep in. A nearby restaurant was commissioned to feed us. We were given the local community hall and all commerce and establishments were closed two nights in a row for our event.

When they saw that we were in with the local leadership people began to come up and whisper in my ear that they liked to listen to our radio station and to my messages. They told me that I was the only missionary or preacher to ever have been invited to speak publicly to this town and that even now they could not believe that this was really happening.

The first night we almost had a mishap. The stage was made of rough planks strewn over the top of several rows of 55 gallon gasoline drums. As our musicians and singers went ahead with the program a huge guerrilla showed up with a big bottle of *aguardiente* (firewater) in his hand and jumped onto the platform. He proceeded to dance his version of a Russian Cossack dance to our music while he grabbed a microphone and said that he would give his bottle of *aguardiente* to anyone who could out dance him.

Soon the platform was filled with guerrillas trying to win the impromptu dance contest. I thought the whole platform was going to come down! Several of us really started to pray.

I was sitting just to one side of the platform in front of the crowd beside the sound engineer, Fernando. All of a sudden, the big guerrilla with the bottle of *aguardiente* jumped off the platform and came over to me. I had boxes of books, Bibles and tapes under the sound booth which I was discretely giving out to people. Many of them put *Rescue the Captors* down the inside of their black rubber boots. I handed a book to the big fierce guerrilla who turned out to be named Yuri. He took it with both hands and began to weep.

The more I spoke with him, the more he wept. Every time I handed him more of our materials it seemed to affect him more and more. He began to say that he had listened to me for years on the radio and that a battle had been going on in his heart. Now, God had touched him and he was going to give up drinking. In fact, he said, between huge sobs that the money he had been saving up to get drunk with that weekend he would spend instead on us.

Yuri motioned to some of his men and in a few minutes we were served the biggest and tastiest barnyard fed chickens that I have ever seen before or since. After a while, Nelson Rey, another of our singers came over and whispered in my ear, "Martín, I think it is OK. I think he is weeping out of happiness!"

I continued sharing with Yuri who now seemed quite sober and kept passing out literature from time to time as the opportunity arose. Later in the evening we almost lost control again as people once more began to turn things into a wild dance.

Just as things began to really get out of hand, tragedy struck. A woman who had been dancing in a frenzy suddenly passed out in the middle of the hall. The guerrilla leaders stopped the event, medics were called in but to no avail. The woman had dropped dead. She was carried out, and a funeral service commenced for her in the next house down the street. With the party quieted down, our team began to play some more serious, heartfelt songs. The tragic moment left everyone vulnerable and receptive. I was able to openly distribute and effectively pass out our materials to all the guerrilla leaders present.

Giving out Rescue the Captors
and other materials to a guerrilla

CHAPTER 17

The next day, I had a bit of a scare because for quite a while we lost little Russell, my ten year old son who was with us. After combing the town for hours looking for him, we finally found out what happened. It turned out that someone started a shooting contest with air rifles down the main street of town. People had to pay a certain amount in order to take a shot, and whoever hit the bull's-eye would get all the money.

Little Russell found a friend about his age and between the two of them they managed to stake little Russell for a shot in the contest. Russell hit the bull's-eye, and the two kids got all the money. Then they found a video game arcade and proceeded to spend the money playing video games. They had been at it for quite a while when we finally found them.

The next night went well, but we were unable to return to Puerto Lleras because it was the day of the swearing in ceremony for the first term of President Alvaro Uribe, and the guerrillas reacted all over Colombia. The ferry over the Ari Ari River was closed in the midst of bombs and gunfire. We safely returned to Bogotá in the midst of all the turmoil by a different road.

The new government began to drive back the guerrilla forces. Paramilitary also began to cut off supplies going into guerrilla controlled cocaine producing areas. Soon the guerrilla leadership of Villa

La Paz called us up and asked for our help. They wanted to have what they called a "Peace Forum". Everyone was invited, they wanted the

The Ari Ari River ferry

press, human rights groups, NGO's and all of us to come and have a massive "peace" rally.

I began to go back and forth through all the road blocks of soldiers, paras, and guerrillas to help them with all the invitations. On each trip, I took as many boxes of books and Bibles as I discreetly could and stashed them in the bedrooms under the beds in the house of Zacarias who was opening up more and more to the Gospel. We also began to plug the rally on our radio station.

On one key trip to a parallel event, I had the red Suburban loaded with materials, and it lit on fire driving down one of the main streets of Bogotá. Due to the

We passed out thousands and thousands of books and Bibles in Villa la Paz

smoke, we had to pile out of the vehicle until the electrical fire burned itself out. The wiring to the alternator and to all the lights had all burned up. Carlos Mario, who was with me, said, "What do we do now?" There was no time to fix the car because if we did we would miss the event. I looked at Carlos and said, "I am going to turn the key and if it starts we are going to keep going." The old Suburban started and there was enough juice in the battery to get us where we needed to go!

On the day of the big event, the guerrillas brought close to seven thousand people into the small town. For some reason Amnesty International, Human Rights Watch, The International Red Cross and other important entities that had been carefully invited never showed up. We were then asked to give three messages to the huge crowd. Several reporters were present including Steve Salisbury who wrote an article about us in the Washington Times.

The townspeople had butchered more than 20 steers and had made roast meat for thousands of people. In the midst of the festivities, we pulled all the books out of the back bedroom of the house of Zacarias and passed out close to ten thousand items. People told me that they had not seen a Bible in twenty years and swarmed all over our vehicle trying to get one.

A few weeks later, we did a similar event on the opposite side of the township of Puerto Lleras in the hamlet of Casibare, which was central to the paramilitary. We began to air the content of these events on the radio so that each side of the conflict could hear how their enemies were responding to the Gospel.

At Casibare we also passed out large quantities of our camouflage Bibles and other materials to the paramilitary. Their leaders, known as Jorge Pirata (George, the Pirate) and Cuchillo (Knife) were very open to our ministry and allowed us free reign just like John 40 on the other side of the river. As in the case of John 40, I had also known them for many years.

Literature distribution at Casibare

Some reporters also went with us on this trip. Canadian Evangelist, Len Carter, gave a powerful message that had quite an effect on backslidden Christians who had become involved in the cocaine industry while continuing to run the local church in Casibare. This problem had be-

Marina and I with Jean and Sandy Bergeron

come prevalent in most cocaine producing areas. Christians who decided to go with the tide would prosper economically but lose the cutting edge and effectiveness of their witness.

One day our Canadian reps, Jean and Sandy Bergeron came to visit us from Vancouver. They spent a few days in Bogotá and then decided to come with me and see Lomalinda. After getting them through the mountains and over the rough road, my wife wanted us to spend a few days out at the radio station. I felt impressed in my spirit to return with them immediately to Bogotá.

We left Lomalinda in the morning, and after a couple hours, I pulled over at a gas station to let them take a break. I noticed a couple of Yamaha 125 dirt bikes half a block away that probably belonged to the guerrillas, but we took our time and had coffee and breakfast.

Meanwhile, the leader of the guerrilla patrol was frantically trying to contact Chaddy. He finally got through and asked if he could contact me. "Tell your brother to move on," he implored, "I have orders to do something, but I am not allowed to proceed until your brother and his friends are completely out of my area." Chaddy told the man that he had no way to contact me. He would just have to wait until we decided to leave on our own. "Where is Martín anyway?" Chaddy asked. "He is parked at a gas station right in front of me!" was the reply.

After about forty-five minutes, unaware of the situation at hand, we pulled out of the gas station and continued to the paved highway where the town of Fuente de Oro was located. As soon as we crossed through the town the guerrillas attacked it with bombs and gas cylinders. They semi-destroyed the police station and reportedly kidnapped the mayor. Ours was probably the last civilian vehicle to transit that road for many days. The entire area was sealed off, but we were out the other side and were able to put Jean and Sandy safely on their flight out of Bogotá a couple days later for Miami. Over the years we have gone through situations like this and time and time again the Lord has always been faithful.

Here I am with my mother, our sound crew and Canadian Evangelist Len Carter

Rescue the Captors II

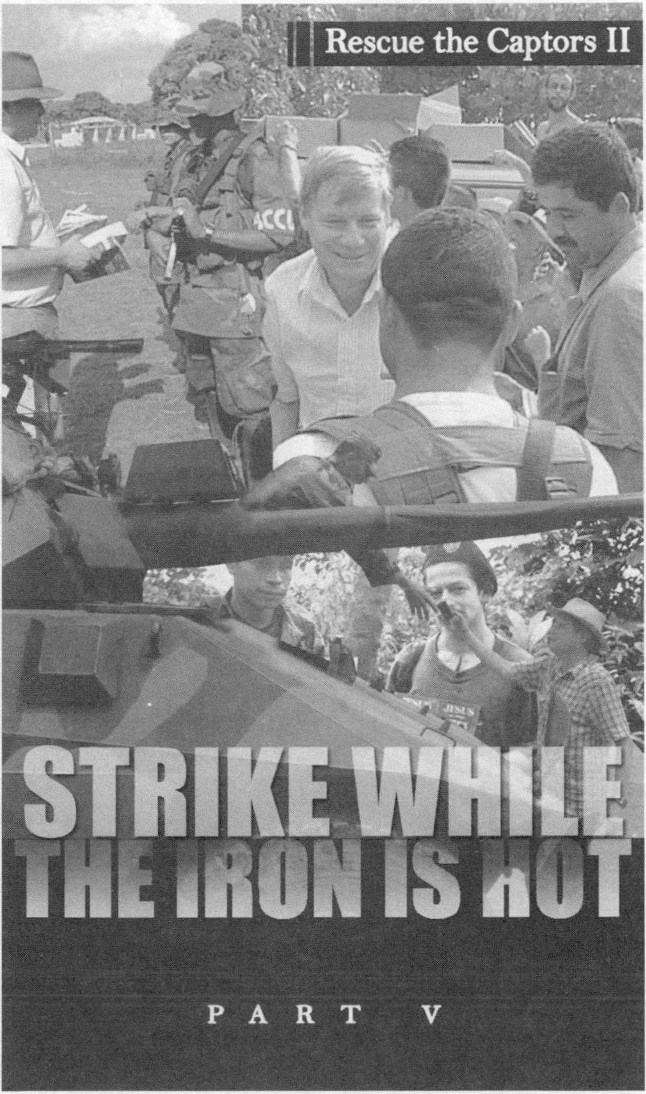

STRIKE WHILE
THE IRON IS HOT

PART V

PART V

Many guerrilles have been touched by
<u>Jesus, A Friend for Terrorists</u>,
by Richard Wurmbrand

CHAPTER 18

September, 2002

*I*n the midst of all the uncertainty and confusion surrounding the collapse of the demilitarized zone to the south of us, paramilitary vigilantes began to enter our area in force. One day a twenty-one year old black man named Victor, commander of 400 mercenaries, came to our radio station with his body guards. He introduced himself and then cordially invited me to come and address his men whenever it was "convenient". Remembering my father's advice to always, "strike while the iron is hot" I replied, "How about now?"

Victor, in a show of confidence and bravado dispatched his body guards and got in the Suburban with me. As we drove back into the hills towards his camp, some of the local people thought my wife and I were being taken out to be shot for having been too friendly with the guerrillas!

At Victor's camp he proceeded to bring out his men in groups so that I could speak to them. After a while I began to see that Victor was getting very uncomfortable with my messages. He was sitting in a lawn chair next to my wife, Marina, and I could see that he was really starting to squirm. Finally, as I continued to speak of the evils of the cocaine traffic and the fallacy of "just following orders" he could take it no more.

Turning to my wife, he asked, "Do you like papaya?" She nodded, "Yes". There was a papaya tree just behind me and to my right full of papayas. In the middle of my discourse to the men all-of-a-sudden Victor lowered his M-16 and pointed at the papaya tree. I just barely had time to take a quick step back out of the line of fire when he pulled the trigger and timbered the tree. He gestured to one of his men to load the entire papaya tree into the back of our Suburban. Then he motioned to me to continue with my message.

I did not give in but continued to press them all strongly for repentance until Victor stood up and told me that I had said enough. He turned to his men and in a vivid voice filled with a tinge of rage said that if any of them were in agreement with my message that they could get in my car and go home with me. I thanked him for the papayas and my wife and I went back to the radio station. It was a long time before I was asked to speak to another group of paramilitary. Yet I was glad I stuck to my guns, because now they all knew what I stood for.

A few days later, I returned to Lomalinda to find one of our Christian neighbors almost in a nervous breakdown. Paramilitary forces had not only commandeered his house, but they were torturing and killing people in the woods behind his pasture adjacent to our radio station. Then they would return to his house and wash the blood off their hands in his bathroom while they expected his wife to wait on them and make breakfast!

Shortly after this, the commanding army general for our area came to see me and asked if I would give him permission to use one of our houses. He wanted to set up his forward command post at our radio station. Noticing that the paramilitary disappeared when the army showed up, I told General Saveedra that he was most welcome. Not only was this the solution for the problems of our neighbor, but I was also given preferential treatment at all the army road blocks in the entire area. Now I could go into the secret war planning and situation room that the general had set up and plan how to carry out the most effective Bible and radio distribution to the troops as well as to the paramilitary and the guerrillas!

One day after an extensive all night journey through extremely dangerous territory where I had been passing out materials to all sides I got a

Zacarias

frantic phone call from Zacarias. Paramilitary had him surrounded at Villa La Paz and he wanted me to come out and get him. He said he wanted to leave the guerrilla movement and join me, but that I had to hurry before they killed him. After checking in with the army, I took off for Villa La Paz with my wife and my brother-in-law, Javier. Unknown to me, I had a serious enemy half way out there in the little town of Caño Rayado.

It was this same guerrilla, nicknamed Pitufo (the Smurf) who had closed the churches in Puerto Lleras. He had also been getting more and more irate about my radio messages and literature distribution. He sent word with my neighbor (the same one who had just had the problem with the paramilitary) that if I ever went back over there he was going to do me in. Oblivious to the danger, I headed right for his town on my way to Villa La Paz to rescue Zacarias. Later, when I asked the neighbor why he never warned me, he said that he saw that the hand of the Lord was on me, so he did not want to scare me off since I was being such a blessing to everyone over there!

As we were arriving at Caño Rayado, some of the general's men captured someone that I believe was Pitufo or some of his men. Thinking that they were local drug growers, they confiscated their weapons and let them go. We continued on to Villa La Paz driving right through the middle of the war. Troops, paramilitary and guerrillas were fully deployed fighting one another along the way.

Homemade explosives, made out of urea and diesel fuel were buried in five gallon plastic containers all along the road. The guerrillas would set them off if the army or paramilitary attempted to use the roads. As the sun

Giving materials to a tank crew

came out and it became a scorching hot day, many of these charges began to spontaneously explode as we drove along, at times rocking our vehicle. We got Zacarias and his family into the Suburban and started back home. Halfway back, as we were passing the first army outpost the captain came out and flagged us down.

"I want you to do me a favor," he asked. I can't use the road because of all the explosives, and I am only supplied by helicopter every couple weeks. Since I confiscated the weapons of those guys from Caño Rayado the law only grants me 72 hours to turn them in to my superior. I wonder if you could take these guns to the general for me." Marina said, "We won't have anything to do with guns!" But knowing how difficult it would be to cross all seven army lines ahead with Zac and his family on board and the possibility of being identified by guerrilla deserters who had joined the opposite side, I said, "No problem. If you will call ahead and open all the road blocks for us, we will do as you say."

The captain handed me the guns and ammunition. I gave one to my brother-in-law and kept two for myself. We went down the road to Caño Rayado and I glanced out and saw what looked like poor Pitufo and his friends; they had been really mad at us, but now they had no weapons. We had their guns. I really felt sorry for them. We whizzed by and then went safely through seven army road blocks with Zacarias and family hunkered down in the back of the Suburban. *Rescue the Captors* began to take on a new depth of meaning for me.

Several weeks later, Pitufo was killed by the army when he attempted to run through their roadblock on a motorcycle and throw a hand grenade at the soldiers. The grenade was a dud, and one of the soldiers shot him.

In the midst of the war zone
this pastor flagged us down and
we loaded him up with Bibles

CHAPTER 19

Some time later, Zacarias and I decided to go back to Villa La Paz and see how things were going. My sixteen-year-old daughter, Alethia, somehow got into the car with us. The army operation had fizzled out a bit when the captain who had given us the weapons tried to take a bridge and got shot in the leg. This gave the guerrillas opportunity to regroup.

When we crossed into guerrilla territory, I noticed that they had a real bad attitude towards us at their first road block. When we got to Villa La Paz Zacarias was told that he must stay and speak with Nacho, the guerrilla area commander. They said Alethia and I were free to go. However, they were playing cat and mouse with us.

Back at the command post of General Saveedra the radio operators were startled to intercept an order from Nacho to detain Alethia and myself with shoot to kill authorizations if we attempted to escape. I had no way of knowing that at the time, but fearing for Alethia, I managed to get us through the first guerrilla road block. Then an armed guerrilla on a motorcycle got in front of us and we were forced back to Villa La Paz under escort.

Alethia stayed calm even when I was separated from her and taken to meet with Nacho. The ordeal lasted for a couple days and a severe rain storm delayed my "trial". But something happened in the meantime. I believe that someone must have called Nacho because when I met with him he was cool but quite cordial. He was very upset about the literature that we had been distributing in his area and about the people that I had taken out of Villa La Paz in my vehicle. I was prohibited from any further distribution of literature by order of the entire guerrilla leadership of that front.

Finally, I was reunited with Alethia and allowed to leave. I introduced Alethia to Nacho and Nacho rose to the occasion as a charming gentleman. Zacarias was even allowed to return with us. Later Zac told me that he had never seen Nacho behave so well. We could not figure out what had gotten into him. Yet I had definitely gotten the picture. Our immediate distribution of literature and personal ministry south of the river to the 43rd front was most definitely cut off.

The results of our literature, personal visits and radio messages had obviously caused the fur to fly among the guerrilla leadership. Alethia, Zac, and I had been extremely fortunate to get out of there alive. The Lord had obviously given me exactly the right words to say to Nacho. I began thinking over the implications of all this on our way home.

In the late evening, Alethia, Zacarias and I

crossed the ferry over the Ari Ari River into Puerto Lleras. The ferry was scheduled to be removed from the river for several weeks for maintenance and this was the last day of operation. As I drove through town my friend, Gilberto, ran out into the street and flagged me down. "I have a phone call for you," he yelled.

Steve Salisbury took this picture of me with one of Nacho's men

Entering his shop I picked up the phone. On the other end of the line there was a vaguely familiar voice which I knew must be yet another guerrilla commander. "I want to know if you can come up and meet with me tomorrow. I have sent a lady to the house of your brother-in-law who will show you the way. We need to know right now if you will come."

In the type of ministry I am in, we must continually make decisions on the spur of the moment that may very well have life or death implications for us or for others. I know that my own feelings are not trustworthy yet I have an ever growing appreciation of God's feelings.

Even though that fateful evening I did not per-

Passing out literature at check points along the road

sonally care if I ever met with another guerrilla commander, I found myself giving the caller an immediate and confident response. "Yes, I will go. You can count on me." The voice on the phone was incredulous, "Are you sure? Will you really come?" "Yes, I will leave as early as possible in the morning," I assured him.

Alethia, who had come running into the building behind me said, "Dad, where are you going in the morning? I am coming too." "Oh no you are not," I replied, "This is getting way too dangerous".

By morning, Alethia had worn me down. She reminded me of all the times that the Lord had kept us safe. She told me that she was also part of this ministry and that the Lord had just got done using us as a team. In the morning she eagerly got into the car and somehow, I did not have the heart to make her get back out. I just said, "We will have to be very careful how we explain all this to your mother when we get home."

Soon Carlos Mario, Zacarias, Alethia and myself found ourselves in the company of our Indian lady guide, heading up what we now fondly refer to as *The Mountain*. Crowned with some of the most rugged peaks in the eastern Andes ,this particular piece of real estate consists of a labyrinth sixty kilometers across and rises to 4,120 meters (13,667 ft.) above sea level. It is known by the locals as *La Brava* (the hard, difficult, or furious one). Containing some of the most extreme vertical terrain in the world, this area was not penetrated even by pre-Colombian Indian civilizations.

We made it past army checkpoints, paramilitary guard posts, over rickety bridges, past way too many burned out farms and deserted villages and then up the side of the vast and seemingly impossible mountain with the Suburban spinning and clawing its way up the almost impossible slope in four wheel drive. After a while we picked up two guerrillas who helped us continue until it was obvious that our trusty vehicle could go no further. I somehow managed to get it turned around and pointed back down the hill. Alethia and Zac mounted mules, while I shouldered my backpack, put on my hiking boots, and we followed our guides into the beautiful yet intimidating unknown.

The guerrillas ready the mules

Shining waterfalls, crystal streams, towering forests teeming with wildlife: all this in the midst of the longest, ongoing, internal conflict in recent world history. After a couple hours traversing this majestic wonderland, we came to a remote farm house next to a wooden watch tower built over a stable. More guerrillas, many of them female, came gliding out of the shadows, and I soon found myself face to face with the author of the phone call.

Short, wiry, fatherly, with pronounced Cauca Indian features, I recognized him even though a lot of time had gone by. "Noel Perez! I have not seen you in almost fifteen years! Ever since that trip down the river when Giovani flagged us down." Noel introduced me to Eduardo, who was another important commander, to his wife, Andrea, and to the others.

Noel, Eduardo, and I climbed up into the wooden watch tower and talked until late in the evening. Alethia spent some time with the other young people but then insisted on sitting beside me in the tower.

Noel told me that he had been listening to my radio messages for quite some time and that he had finally decided to contact me. He realized that many of the guerrillas had been rash and imprudent, causing serious problems which had led to the present state of affairs. "We don't have many friends that we can really count on," he sadly told me. "I know that you don't agree with some of the things that we do, and I know that some of us don't agree with your beliefs, but I wonder if there are areas of common interest where we can work together. I would like for your friends to be my friends, and for my friends to be your friends, irregardless of ideological lines."

I told Noel and Eduardo that I do not believe in "movements" or even in "institutions" but that I do believe in friendship with sincere individuals. Sometimes our background and even our terminology can drive us apart. The guerrilla movement claims to be atheist yet at the same time their anthem calls for Justice and for Truth.

Those who to the best of their conscience seek justice and truth are really seeking God even if they are confused in their perception and terminology. On the other hand, some of those who claim to represent God are hypocrites like the Pharisees of Jesus day. If the guerrillas reject hypocrites claiming to be Christians, then that is definitely along the lines of justice and truth, but we must be very careful not to throw out the baby with the bathwater. The

Alethia with some of Noel's men

fact that there are an abundance of hypocrites does not mean that there are no real Christians or that Jesus Christ is not real.

From time to time Alethia would help me comment on something. We told them that Jesus stood up against the corrupt system of this world as a true revolutionary, yet without resorting to the weapons of this world. Jesus uses the truth as his weapon. Jesus is The Truth. Jesus is still fighting revolutionary battles against corruption in and through each and any of us that are willing to give up our own way to go His way. The light and the truth of God are infinitely more powerful than the corruptible weapons of the guerrillas, the paramilitary. the Colombian Army, or even the United States. True Christians are also in a revolutionary war against corruption and injustice, but we do not need to use guns and explosives because we have something much more powerful and much more effective.

The guerrillas finally put us to bed on the floor of the farmhouse. I slept back to back with Alethia. We had one thin wool blanket to help fend off the icy cold that soon began to blow down the side of

The Mountain fresh from the realm of the high alpine meadows known in Colombia as *El Páramo*.

I arose at 4 AM stiff with cold and pulled on my boots. Like the guerrillas who were already up, we had slept in our clothes. Eduardo was in the wooden watchtower intensely casing the area with a pair of good binoculars. As the dawn began to spread and the icy mist from the mountain retreated, Eduardo found himself face to face through his binoculars with paramilitary just a few hundred yards away who were also casing us with their binoculars through the mist!

Fortunately there was a bit of a valley filled with dense brush between us and the paramilitary who appeared to be forming a skirmish line. The guerrillas quickly packed their gear and deployed into the shadows to reinforce the perimeter around us. Andrea and several other women were in the farm kitchen making breakfast. Just as breakfast was being served, the shooting started. Rapid bursts from automatic weapons reverberated up and down the valley.

Bible distribution to the paramilitary. Foto by Steve Salisbury

Carlos Mario and Zac thought that we

A guerrilla girl makes us breakfast

should forget about returning to our vehicle which was down the valley in the direction of the paramilitary. They wanted to immediately retreat up the mountain with the guerrillas. Noel and Eduardo, seated at the breakfast table with the four of us, waited intently for my reply. I knew deep inside that everything I had told them the night before was now being put to the test.

Fighting the urge to panic, I drew a deep breath and paused as if I had all the time in the world. I looked at Alethia and knew that I could count on her. So I turned to Carlos Mario and Zac and said, "You are free to do as you please, but Alethia and I are going to eat breakfast and then walk down the valley, find the Suburban, and drive home." I managed to eat most of my breakfast. Alethia made a valiant effort to eat some of hers. Carlos Mario and Zac were too nervous to eat much of anything as the sounds of battle continued.

Noel also ate his breakfast, glanced at me, and then said, "If you go back down that valley you are on your own. I will not be able to offer you mules or guides." I smiled and reassured him that we would be fine. Then I said goodbye, shouldered my backpack and started down the trail with Alethia. After some hesitation Zac and Carlos Mario reluctantly followed. At a signal from Noel, one of the guerrillas went with us to the bridge over the first stream to make sure we took the right trail and then melted into the jungle.

And so came into being what became known as the "Friends Plan" of Noel.

Back at the forward command post of General Saveedra at Lomalinda, there was a flurry of activity. When the army radio monitors intercepted the orders from Nacho to detain us with authorization to shoot to kill, the general picked up on our emergency and began to work on trying to save us. He had been able to breath a sigh of relieve when his check points finally informed him that Alethia and I had been able to safely leave the guerrilla area to the south of our radio station. The general had expected me to stop by the next morning and tell him all about our close call with Nacho.

The next day, however, to his amazement and consternation, the general found out from his intelligence staff that we had headed west up into *The Mountain* where he also knew there was an intense battle going on between the paramilitary and the guerrillas. Deeply concerned for our safety he had another unit of soldiers to the north of Lejanias which he now must have ordered to move forward. As these soldiers from the Colombian Army moved forward it may have caused the paramilitary to back off to the next ridge apparently trying to avoid a confrontation.

The effect of whatever happened left the immediate area in front of us clear so we came down *The Mountain* right between the army and the paramilitary, got in the Suburban, which was just as we had left it, and began the drive home. Soon we passed through the army lines. They waved us through and I could tell that they must have been ordered to watch out for us. Quite a few miles further down the road we were stopped by several vehicles flashing their headlights. It was General Saveedra himself! I was greeting with a huge bear hug and ushered into the back of the general's command car to tell him all about my recent adventures.

A Paez Indian asks me for
literature and for copies of some
of our radio programs

Rescue the Captors II

¡La Señal que Cambia tu Vida! 1530 AM
Alcaravan Radio

Escucha

MARFIL 88.8 STEREO
Ondas de Paz

Escucha
En las ondas Cortas
6010
La Voz de Tu Conciencia

Fuerza de Paz

THE LIGHT OF THE TRUTH

PART VI

PART VI

The boat used to be called
La Diabla (the She-Devil)

CHAPTER 21

March, 2003

The fighting intensified in the area of Villa La Paz and Puerto Toledo. Both places were reduced to ghost towns. Some of the yards and streets were overtaken by the jungle. Army garrisons patrolled the ruins of these once prosperous cocaine producers.

In the midst of many battles, the men led by General Saveedra confiscated a river launch named *La Diabla* (The She-Devil), which had belonged to the guerrillas, and donated it to us. We had quite a time getting it out of Puerto Toledo and back to Puerto Lleras. *La Diabla* was painted dull red and had a devil insignia on it complete with pitchfork. We fixed it up, installed a bathroom, painted it white and green, and renamed the 70 ft. boat *La Luz de La Verdad* (The Light of the Truth).

We decided to make a maiden voyage for this boat down the Ari Ari River and then up the Guayabero River to La Macarena. This would take us right through the thick of the conflict. With a crew of 24, including my wife, Marina, and 3 of our

4 children: Lisa, Russell Jr., and our youngest, Dylan, we sailed down river from Puerto Lleras. We planned to pick up 10 tons of books, Bibles, and supplies at Puerto Rico thirty miles downstream where the river was deep enough in the dry season for us to navigate with a load.

On the second day of our voyage, we arrived in Puerto Rico at noon. As arrangements were made to refuel and load our cargo, disaster struck and the boat blew up. The blast threw Zacarias, who was the motorman, into the water leaving him with moderate burns on his hands and feet. His three year old grandson, Jason, however, was seriously burned. Alex, our video engineer, jumped back into the fire and saved the boy. We took him to the town hospital and made arrangements for a charter airplane to medivac him to Villavicencio. We were able to put out the fire by shoveling sand into the boat. Most of our gear and supplies were burned up, but the books and Bibles had not yet been loaded and were safe.

No sooner had we gotten through the first stages of this emergency when the guerrillas attacked the town. Most of our people were caught in the cross fire, yet all emerged unscathed. After five or six rockets hit the hospital where Jason was sent, it had to be evacuated in the middle of the firefight and the medivac flight was unable to land. Several hundred soldiers, a hundred policemen and an undetermined number of guerrillas, possibly under the command of Nacho, were all shooting it out with major weapons, and we were right in the middle. I was able to account for everyone except for our son, little Russell, who was lost.

Desperately I began to make my way back into the cross fire towards the beach beside our boat to see if he was there. Just before I was about to run out into the thick of it, Russell was found safe and alive. Someone had found him running disoriented and they stuck him down into a cement water tank, the safest place they could find.

Rein-forcements arrived and the shooting stopped. We were able to get the medivac flight to come back and land to evacuate the burned child

It took a lot of work to convent the "She Devil" into the Light of the Truth

who, for the second time that day, survived without any serious consequences. Several others had to be treated for shrapnel from the rockets. I decided to send half my crew home to lower costs and risks and attempt to repair the boat and continue.

When word got out over the radio of our plight people from three municipalities pitched in to help us. The mayors provided us with more fuel; the merchants gave us gear and food. The Marfil school teachers association took up a large collection for us. A local shop repainted the boat. Zacarias, after a brief stay in the hospital, decided that he could continue. We loaded the books and Bibles and within 48 hours we were on our way down river.

This trip took us through horrible scenes of devastation and despair. We were able to minister to thousands of needy people. Our voyage went right through the center of the territory of the 7th front of the FARC, which had kidnapped me almost twenty years before. We passed right in front of the mouth of Caño La Tigrera, the stream where I had been held hostage for several months in 1983, and we were able to saturate the entire area with copies of *Rescue The Captors*.

Towns like La Carpa, Puerto Nuevo and others, all the way up to La Macarena, were flooded with Bibles and literature. But when we got to Puerto Cachicamo, the capital city of the guerrillas in that area, it appeared that we were in trouble with the guerrillas. Someone had been spreading lies and rumors about us, and it looked like there would be serious consequences.

After a few minutes, Gentil Duarte, commander of the 7th front, appeared seemingly out of nowhere and called me aside to ask for an explanation. I told him about Noel Perez and the "Friends Plan" and then named all the guerrillas that I knew who were friends. Gentil thought for a moment and then said, "Those men are all friends of mine too!" Then he said, "I heard the story about when someone like you was kidnapped years ago, but you look way too young for it to have been you." I gave him some copies of my book and one of the flags of the "Friends Plan" that was unfurled on our boat. I was told that as long as I could vouch for everyone on board that we would be allowed to continue.

Along the way, there were some severe rapids on the river that could not be navigated in the dry season. When we got to them, the Lord sent rain right in the middle of what was normally the driest period of the year, and we were able to go up and down the rapids with no problem. Further up the river, we were detained for a few hours by a guerrilla patrol boat while they checked us out. When they finally let us proceed, I asked them why they had stopped us. "It is because this is a strange boat that we did not recognize", they answered. I had to chuckle to myself. *La Diabla* had made many journeys up this river and was well known to them. Even Zac and Ramiro from our crew used to work for them, and they didn't seem to recognize them either!

I began to notice that we did not have very good radio coverage over much of this river. Our FM signal from Lomalinda was too weak. AM and short wave came in a bit at night, but I longed to be able to send a clear radio signal that would enter these places like gangbusters. We passed over a dozen towns and villages that had no churches and little or no witness. No one had ever seen a missionary or even a Bible unless they had been fortunate enough to travel outside the vast area under guerrilla control. This river went on and on like this for hundreds and hundreds of miles and there are dozens of rivers like this in Colombia.

The Light of the Truth navegates deep within guerrilla territory with a full load of materials

CHAPTER 22

May, 2003

Back at Lomalinda I made every effort to beef up our radio transmitters. Every few months I would go up and see how Noel was doing. On each trip I would distribute our literature and radios all along the way. Noel helped me pick a good spot for a mountain radio repeater. The only problem was that he did not have complete control over the area I needed. Noel suggested that I ask permission from the paramilitary as well.

Every trip to see Noel was quite a sobering experience. Sometimes we had to drive around dead bodies that had lain in the open, unburied for months. At other times, we wound up in the middle of a fire fight or in towns that had been abruptly abandoned by occupants who were forced to flee on extremely short notice. I found dozens of schools that had been destroyed or abandoned along with small rural medical centers called *puestos de salud*. It was extremely rare to find a church building. Not even a Roman Catholic Church building. All the people, however, seemed thrilled to be able to listen to our messages over the radio.

I went to see the paramilitary commander near El Dorado. His name was Julian. When I told him what I wanted to do and where I wanted to do it he immediately offered to help. By the time I got back with my radio equipment, he had twenty men ready to carry everything. My engineers installed it all in an abandoned school building riddled with bullet holes on top of a high ridge. On one occasion, I was very close to a firefight, and I was instructed to walk only down the center of the main path because everywhere else was mined.

On my way up to check on my transmitter every few weeks, I would pass out books and Bibles to the paramilitary who had camps all along the way. One day, I passed out materials to all the men. I came back a few days later and twenty of them had been killed in a fight with the guerrillas. It was apparent that Noel and his group were also taking severe losses.

At first, Noel told me that he was doing OK and that in spite of all the pressure from the paramilitary and the government that he had everything he needed. Then one day he broke down and said, "We are in serious trouble. We have no food, no medicine. We can't even take care of our wounded." Then Noel said something that just about floored me, "I wonder if you can get me the phone number of Julian? I need to talk to him."

Somehow, I had never heard about the Catholic priest named Julian who had been run out of the area by the guerrillas a couple years before. Julian had been in charge of a Catholic boarding school on one side of *The Mountain*. The guerrillas had decided to apologize to Father Julian for their bad behavior and attempt to coax him back into the area with the hope that he might be able to bring them food and medicine.

Oblivious to this, I went down and found Julian, the commander of the paramilitary and told him that the guerrillas were asking for his phone number. I had been witnessing to him (the same as to Noel) about overcoming evil with good and about reaching out even to his enemies. He gave me his phone number, and after a few weeks I was able to give the phone number to Noel. A few days later, Noel called the number I gave him and asked to speak with "Father" Julian.

Neither the guerrillas nor the paramilitary speak very explicitly on the phone, knowing that their conversations are probably being intercepted by the government. It is more or less standard procedure with the paramilitary that when you call and want to talk to the boss you tell whoever answers that you want to speak to their "father". Noel called, a girl answered, and Noel asked for *Father* Julian. The girl without a question gave the phone to *Commander* Julian.

Noel said, "I am the number two of the 26th front and I need to talk with you. When can you come up and see me?"

Without missing a beat, Julian replied, "How about Thursday? But I am not coming alone. I know that Martín is your friend, and he is also my friend. I will come if you line it up for Martín to take me."

All of a sudden I began to get phone calls from both Noel and Julian. Julian wanted to know if it was safe for him to go visit Noel with me and what I thought about it, and if I was in a position to guarantee his safety. Noel told me to line up the trip to see him with the fellow who just called me. I asked Noel if he was sure he knew what he was doing and if the other guerrilla commanders were in agreement. He assured me that this was the case and asked me to tell the fellow that we would "guarantee his safety". I mentioned that this all seemed a bit risky to me, thinking that if anything went wrong the paramilitary might go after me or my family. So I asked Noel what he was planning to say to this guy.

Noel answered that, "Since they have authority almost everywhere" (Noel was thinking of the Catholic Church), "we want them to state their position regarding all the things that are happening around here." (I was thinking paramilitaries and trying to put this all together, but then the phone went dead and Noel never called back).

Since I had been ministering to both sides about loving your enemies, praying for those who persecute you, and overcoming evil with good, I hoped that maybe the message was sinking in so I went ahead with the trip. At the last minute Noel asked me to pick up a lady in Villavicencio on my way out and bring her along. At the time I was not sure who the lady was, but I could see that she was scared to death at even the thought of going out there. She turned out to be his mother-in-law, and I found out later that she had been paranoid that either the army or the paramilitary were going to torture or kill her.

When we approached the command post of Julian early in the morning I ended up driving in there with her in the car because there was no secure place nearby to leave her. As we entered the driveway to the little farm, I noticed a new vehicle full of guys who all piled out and took off running into a banana patch as we came barreling up the lane. I later found out that it was the mayor of a nearby town who was out there trying to make a secret deal with the paramilitary, and they did not want anyone to see them!

After a few minutes, Julian drove up in two stake bed Toyotas loaded with bodyguards. He introduced me to Gabriel, the head of his training institute, and told me that Gabriel would be the one to go with me to handle the negotiation with Noel. Julian wanted to send someone who had not been directly involved in the fighting. The last thing Julian told me was that if anything went wrong, and they did not return Gabriel that he knew where a lot of guerrilla sympathizers were hiding out and that he would kill them all.

Gabriel climbed into the front seat of my Toyota jeep and I introduced him to the lady in the back who said her name was Esperanza. We drove

A typical road

down the road and headed for *The Mountain* in a round about way. When we came to the last army road block, a soldier in a tee shirt with no insignia asked me the names of my companions. I introduced my "good friends" Gabriel and Esperanza. When he asked for their identification papers, the names were completely different!

The army proceeded to do a meticulous three hour search of our vehicle and interrogation of us. Since none of the army had any insignia or ID, I was starting to get a bit worried. Sizing them up by age and demeanor, I decided that one was probably a Captain and the other a Sergeant, so I began calling them by their titles.

This had quite an effect. Then I began to mention the name of their commanding officer who I knew. Finally they drew up a document releasing themselves of all responsibility from anything they may have done to us or anything that might happen to us along the way and made us all sign it.

The last thing the Captain said to me as we all drove down the road headed into guerrilla territory was, "I don't know what you are up to. The guy with you looks like a paramilitary, and I would swear that the lady is a guerrilla sympathizer. I think you are about to get yourselves killed. If you expect to stay alive, I recommend that you get your act together!"

I left the Captain and his Sergeant with a handful of our books and some of our radios and told them that in a lot of places I had been, things had been much worse.

Sometimes it is only a few hundred meters from the army lines to the guerrillas

Chapter 24

*W*hen we got to the base of *The Mountain,* Andrea stepped out of the woods and "Esperanza", who was her mother, got out ,and they both disappeared. Gabriel and I continued in the jeep up the steep slope after I engaged the four wheel drive. Gabriel, about 38 years old, and slightly bald with a short hair cut and a dark tee shirt with a high turtle neck, looked very much like a priest.

About half way to the end of the road, a guerrilla ran out of a pasture and stopped us saying that his commander was coming and wanted to talk to me. The commander, who was about my age, wore the special red beret of an elite guerrilla unit. Gabriel, quickly ran to meet him first and received an *abrazo* (hug) with a very warm welcome. Then I got a bear hug. The commander said, "Do you remember me? I was the kid who ran the outboard motor when you were kidnapped!"

He was the guerrilla called Arnuval in my book,

Rescue The Captors! Now he commanded an entire front. Arnuval said, "I am in a big hurry with my men but I just wanted to greet you and let you know that I listen to your radio messages. What you are saying is the only way out for any of us. You can count on my full support."

Gabriel started to explain who he was, but I stepped sharply on his foot, silencing him. Then I opened the back door of the Toyota and gave Arnuval an armload of Bibles, books and radios. He thanked me profusely and then took off jogging after his men. Gabriel and I continued up the road. Gabriel was thinking, "Wow! They are really taking my visit seriously. This must be the outer ring of security for our meeting, and they sent this top commander and about two hundred guys!"

When we got to the end of the road Gabriel, who was in perfect shape, took off first and made it to Noel way ahead of me. By the time I got there they were sitting behind the house in plastic lawn chairs, and the guerrillas had piled all their weapons off to one side.

Gabriel had obviously received a royal welcome. I got in on the tail end of a speech that Noel was making to Gabriel. Noel recapped a bit for my benefit. He was saying that the guerrillas had made many mistakes. They had even killed innocent people and done a lot of injustice. Now they were in trouble and needed help. Noel, after making his confession to the "priest" waited for Gabriel to speak.

Gabriel said, "I am really glad to see how repentant you are. This will help to make my job easy. I represent the Centauros paramilitary group, and we are prepared to offer you money for each rifle and for each man that turns himself in. You can count on me to expedite this process."

Noel started to get a funny look on his face and quit being so talkative. Instead he began asking questions. When it was time for lunch, Gabriel and I were served by ourselves in the kitchen while Noel was in the back yard feverishly talking on his radio. After a half hour, two more senior guerrilla commanders strode in. They were Plinio (who I had never met before) and Eduardo. They politely asked me to stay in the kitchen and said that they needed to speak to Gabriel alone.

In the middle of the meeting Esperanza and Andrea arrived out of breath and motioned Noel off to one side. "Gabriel is not really a friend!" Esperanza blurted out, "He is a *parraco*!" This term is slang for paramilitary. "I saw him say goodbye to his friends at the *parraco* headquarters." Noel replied, "How can he be a *parraco*? He came here with our good friend, Martín." "But I know he is a *parraco*. He is a *parraco*!" Esperanza kept insisting. After a while Noel managed to calm her down.

I could see them all sitting there in lawn chairs, but it was too far away for me to make out what was being said. Plinio and Eduardo had also stacked their weapons way off to one side with those of Noel and his men. After about an hour and a half the meeting blew up.

Eduardo started shouting at Gabriel and calling him a *parraco*. Noel got Eduardo off to one side leaving Gabriel with Plinio, who remained calm. Gabriel just kept talking without raising his voice. I could also see that Eduardo seemed to be upset with Noel, telling him in a loud voice that it was all his fault. Noel came over and got me.

Off to one side with Eduardo, he asked me, "I need you to tell me, Martín, exactly what telephone number did you give me; because I asked you for the number of Father Julian from Granada!" I stared at Noel in amazement. "I have never even heard of a Father Julian from Granada," I replied, "I gave you the number of Julian, the paramilitary leader from El Dorado!"

Eduardo, who was mad because he thought that the "priest" had taken sides with the paramilitary, was speechless.

There was a long pause and Noel said, "There has been a huge mistake."

Pointing to Gabriel I said, "Does he know about this mistake? Have you told him yet?"

They both said, "Well, no."

I said, "Good. Don't tell him. This is a golden opportunity for you to talk face to face with your enemy. When will you ever get another chance like this? I think God set this up."

Noel said, "We can talk with him if you will help us. Come, let's all sit down together."

Noel ushered me into a chair next to Gabriel. Eduardo meekly followed and sat back down in his seat.

THE VALLEY OF THE SHADOW OF DEATH

PART VII

PART VII

Entering a previously forbidden realm

CHAPTER 25

The meeting lasted for almost six hours. Eduardo went over all the atrocities committed by the paramilitary. Gabriel politely but firmly reminded them of the abuses and dastardly deeds of the guerrillas. Heads had been cut off, entire families had been burned alive, people had been dragged to death behind vehicles, many elderly had been murdered, and pregnant women had been tortured and killed: each list went on and on.

My impression was that this meeting was very different from the meetings I had attended over the past two decades where the government or the Church had attempted to come to terms with rebel groups in an atmosphere of lies and denial on all sides. What Gabriel and Eduardo were saying had the ring of truth and reality. But there was an immense and humanly impassable breach between the two sides.

Finally Gabriel stopped the litany of charges and

countercharges. He said, "We need to be able to go to a place called, *To Forgive and Forget*. If this is not possible I will go home. I can do no more. I want to ask each one of you if you feel that this is possible. I want to know if, as individuals you want to forgive and forget."

Noel thought for a moment and said, "Yes this is where I want to go. We all need to forgive and forget."

Plinio agreed. We all looked at Eduardo and he turned a bit red in the face and then nodded his head. It was almost dusk. I left the three guerrilla commanders talking with Gabriel on more pleasant terms and went back to the Toyota for two sleeping bags that I had left there. One of the guerrillas went with me, and we had to find our way back into the camp after dark with no flashlight.

Upon our return, I was pleased to see that things still seemed friendly. Gabriel and I slept back to back surrounded by the guerrillas. I say that we "slept" but in reality I don't think that either one of us actually went to sleep. In the morning we all had a

Galcom radio and camouflage Bible being assembled into Truth Pack with parachute

cordial breakfast together, and then Gabriel and I headed back to the Toyota. I gave Gabriel a Bible, and he took it in both hands and held it

Here I am with Noel

open to Psalm 91 until we made it back to the command post of Julian.

Julian listened to our story with great interest. The consensus had been that both sides should repent and start to make amends for all the atrocities. The guerrillas sent word that they were ready to stop stealing cattle, and they wanted to know if the paramilitary would allow essential food and medical supplies to enter their area. Julian thought for a minute and said to me, "We cannot give them food, but if they need medicine or a doctor go ahead."

This led to many "Good Samaritan" trips with my Toyota loaded full of cases of IV bottles, sterile water, rubber gloves, antibiotics, dental supplies and such as I went back and forth between the battle lines helping to save as many lives as possible.

On one memorable occasion, my friend, Dr. Fernando Torres, went with me and we looked after a young guerrilla named Christian who had been shot in the abdomen. Noel, Eduardo, and Plinio wanted to know how much they owed us. A previous doctor they had contracted had charged them 12 million pesos (about $6,000 USD).

Fernando told them, "I have a son about the age of Christian. When I look at him, he reminds me of my son. I could never charge my son."

Fernando walked away and left the three tough guerrilla commanders blinking back tears.

I never charged the guerillas, the soldiers or the paras for any of my help or for my trips. I just kept mentioning to them from time to time the miraculous things that would happen all along the way.

One day I asked Noel, "What do you think about all this? Is it God, or isn't it God?"

Noel looked at me and said, "Martín, all this has got to be God."

Guerrilla Camp

CHAPTER 26

January, 2004

The "Friends Plan" that Noel and I had been implementing continued to blossom. Long time friendships of mine, retired army generals and people in the government began to support our Peace Campaign when they saw that guerrillas were coming to faith in God. Individuals were being touched by God on all sides of the ideological spectrum.

A mutual acquaintance introduced me to Francisco Vergara, a very influential lawyer in Bogotá. "Pacho" Vergara was also an expert pilot and he graciously offered me the use of his Cessna 182 RG. Since my license was not current, Pacho had his instructor, Hector Gonzalez, fly with me to bring me up to date. Hector, a long-lost friend of close to thirty years, was none other than the man who had bought my father's Cessna 170 back in the fall of 1986. This is the airplane on the cover of *Rescue the Captors*.

Pacho had an intense interest in helping to break the stalemate between the guerrillas and the government. He had no end of excellent ideas of how to solve all sorts of problems that were plaguing Colombia and was even an expert legal authority on such themes as the World Court and Extradition to the United States.

In mid 2004, I took Pacho to see Noel. The two of them hit it off and Pacho even gave Noel his special back pack that he had bought to hike through Patagonia the year before. Noel, in turn, lined it up for us to meet with Dario and Lucas, important FARC commanders of the 40th front. Lucas was a doctor and an important ideologue. Dario, the front commander, and I sat back amazed as Pacho and Lucas debated back and forth.

In the mean time, at the paramilitary end of things, Julian was replaced with a new commander named Ramiro. Gabriel remained under Ramiro. Noel called up one day and said that he would like to have another meeting with Gabriel.

I went over to see Ramiro and brought him up to date on all that had transpired previously. Then I told him that in the Bible it says that if your enemy is hungry, we are to feed him. If he is thirsty, we are to give him something to drink. I told him that God's way is to overcome evil with good (Romans 12:20,21). Then I asked him if Gabriel and I could take a load of food, some supplies, and a small electric generator on behalf of the paramilitary organization up to the guerrillas. Ramiro blinked and squirmed but finally gave us the thumbs up.

Gabriel and I took everything in my Toyota up to the end of the trail. Noel sent down all the mules that he could round up. At the end of the trail lived some para-military informants that had been trying to make life miserable for me.

Many campesinos have turned to the Lord

Every time I took a small package up to the guerrillas, they would re-port that I had sent the guerrillas *cuarenta arrobas* (1000 pounds) of supplies in an attempt to get me killed and make a lot of money with their "information". Imagine the look on their faces when we pulled in with a complete load of more than *cuarenta arrobas* along with a deputy paramilitary commander, Gabriel, and made them help us load all this on mules to take to the guerrillas!

When we got there, and the scrawny, malnour-ished guerrillas began to receive the loaded mules, Gabriel took the new generator and handed it to Noel.

Noel took me off to one side, visibly shaken and said, "Help me, I don't know what to say to Gabriel. Nothing like this has ever happened to us before."

I said, "Tell him that you want to make a deal. Tell him that you want all the *campesino* refugees to be able to return to their farms. Tell him that you want both groups, the guerrillas and the paramilitary, to guarantee the safety of the *campesinos* (peasant farmers) and that both groups are to stop killing innocent civilians. From now on the 'military objectives' will only be those that are armed. Let's take the unarmed civilians out of this war."

When Gabriel and I came down off *The Mountain* we were asked to accompany Ramiro to see the top paramilitary commanders of the area, Jorge Pirata and Cuchillo. We were able to personally deliver Noel's proposal to them. *Campesinos* who were refugees in the surrounding towns and cities soon began to trickle back to their farms.

Most of the paramilitary operating out of El Dorado surrendered to the government by 2006. Some of the guerrillas deserted, others moved to new areas. The *campesinos* on *The Mountain* began to have more confidence. Many turned to the Lord as they listened to our radio broadcasts. In the area where we gave Noel the food there had been b l o o d y battles almost on a daily basis. Now there were places

Only the Lord knows how many thousands of people have been transformed by the Gospel

where six months could go by without anyone firing a single shot in anger.

A few weeks after his last trip up *The Mountain* Gabriel was given a one day holiday by Ramiro. Gabriel was unable to handle it. Thinking about all the terrible things which he had participated in and with a conscience that had begun once again to function; Gabriel got drunk and then went AWOL.

In either the paramilitary or the guerrilla organizations, this is punishable by death. Afraid to go back to his unit, Gabriel got on a bus for San Martin and called me. I found him, called Ramiro, and put Gabriel on the phone. He told Ramiro that he did not want to be a paramilitary any longer. Ramiro told him to go in peace. Then I lent Gabriel some money to return to his home town in the center of Colombia. I have not seen him since.

Bridge into a previously forbidden realm

CHAPTER 27

January 2005

Noel, with documents in hand signed by Manuel Marulanda, better known as "Tirofijo", commander and founder of the FARC, wanted to nominate our help to initiate dialogue directly between the FARC military commanders and Colombian Army Generals as the best way to come up with a solution to the conflict. He felt that if those who were involved directly in the fighting could get together and talk that this would be much more productive than dealing with politicians.

A new round of meetings was set up between Noel and Pacho. We were also within an inch of having tacit government permission to have some retired generals meet with FARC military commanders. Now, it seemed to me that it was simply a matter of making careful steps that would inspire confidence on all sides. However, unknown to me, the fact that high ranking guerrillas were starting to speak openly about "faith in God" and that thousands of guerrillas and communist sympathizers were listening to our radio broadcasts had started to ring alarm bells in both the natural as well as the spiritual realm.

Just as we were about to go to this important second meeting with Noel, Zacarias showed up with what appeared to be a sterling invitation for Pacho and myself to meet with a very high ranking guerrilla commander a couple hundred miles to the north of us in a completely different area. After sending messages back and forth, what appeared to be bona fide guarantees were offered. Noel graciously offered to wait while we went to this other meeting first.

After numerous touch and go circumstances, Pacho and I made our way to this new meeting by the end of the first week of February, 2005. His airplane was down for maintenance. We hired a second airplane, and it developed engine trouble. Not only that, but the door jammed with us inside and we were almost unable to get back out. The engine was finally fixed but the weather closed in and we did not know how to operate the GPS on the rented airplane. I had a hand held unit but the maps mysteriously deleted.

We were in the air and about to turn back when the clouds opened up

Pacho says goodby to a FARC commander

and we were able to fly to our destination with bad weather on both sides. Encouraged that so many seemingly impossible factors had all worked out for us, we got in the vehicle that I had sent ahead to drive to the meeting place.

Then we got into what appeared to be our worst nightmare. Armed men, posing as paramilitary, stopped us on the road and took us hostage. Pacho was blindfolded, and I was forced to drive the Toyota way back into the mountains. After a few hours, I was released but Pacho was held hostage for six months. This turned into one of the most difficult and trying times of my life.

Soon we were able to determine that Pacho was really being held by FARC guerrillas of the 28th front who had betrayed us. I returned to the airfield and flew the airplane to the nearest army base and reported what had happened. General Saveedra introduced me by phone to the local commander who was very sympathetic and helpful; yet deep inside I knew that we were in extremely serious trouble that only the Lord could solve.

Alexander Ramirez, my video engineer, had been with me during Pacho's abduction. The next morning, he and I had *breakfast* with the army. Later that day, we went to San Martin and had *lunch* with Jorge Pirata of the paramilitary. In the evening, we hiked way up on *The Mountain* and ate a very late *supper* after 10 PM with some of Noel's guerrilla associates.

After a marathon of activity we finally got the 28th front to admit that they were holding Pacho. They agreed to meet with me. When I eventually got there after facing a long string of contrived and intimidating circumstances (they had even poured blood on the trail and on the gates I had to walk through to attempt to scare me), I recognized the leader as having been one of the kidnappers. Ironically his name was also Julian!

He was uncouth and brash, demanding three and a half million dollars for Pacho.

I told him that this was no way to treat friends.

He replied with a snarl, "There is no such thing as a good American. None of you can ever be trusted as friends!"

His parting line as I left was, "If you don't bring a lot of money, don't bother to come back."

I had attempted to explain to him that his rash action in kidnapping Francisco Vergara was putting in jeopardy a lot of trust and developing relationships that might eventually be able to help solve the conflict, but it was like talking to a stone wall. I told him I would be back and that I would not come alone.

Here I am with Colonel Robinson of the Colombian Army

CHAPTER 28

Zac and I made another marathon trip up to see Noel who wrote a letter to the 28th front. We also had a public relations debacle on our hands as Julian of the 28th front took Pacho's cell phone and proceeded to call, extort and intimidate every name and number in the data bank. Now some of Pacho's important and influential friends were starting to blame me for the kidnapping.

I can remember getting so exhausted to the point that I became disoriented. After a short rest stop I thought I had lost my backpack with the important letter from Noel. I frantically searched beside the trail for over five minutes before realizing, chagrined, that I was still wearing the back pack!

When we finally got down off *The Mountain* my old friend, Hector Gonzalez, was waiting for me in San Martin. He had come to encourage me and to help me recover Pacho. The next day we returned to what is called the ABC triangle (the corner where the Colombian Departments of Arauca, Boyacá and Casanare meet). This was where Pacho was being held. Zac was worried that Julian might do something to me and wanted to go alone with the letter from Noel.

Noting the rather severe and austere bearded face of Hector, I proposed a plan to cut through the stonewalling of Julian. Sometimes the top national guerrilla leadership delegates commanders to check into certain situations. They go not to intervene but simply to come back with a clear report of what was said and done.

I proposed to Zac that we all go to the pool hall and general store where Julian's guerrilla contact men hung out. Zac and Hector could shoot some pool and then we would just naturally start calling Hector, *comandante*. I was sure that Hector would naturally respond well to this, because in Colombia senior pilots are also known as *comandante*.

A half hour into the pool game Hector made a great shot and sank the 15 ball into a side pocket. Zac said, "Great shot, *comandante*."

Soon the guerrilla contact people were discreetly whispering in Zac's ear, asking for the name of the *comandante* who was with us. Zac said he did not know much about him; just that I had known him for a long time.

We overheard one contact man say to the other, "He has to be a very important *comandante*. Just look at his face!"

Instead of having to wait on pins and needles for hours or days, we were told that at our pleasure we could hike up into the jungle and meet with Julian. This time Julian was a bit more cordial. He took the letter from Noel but said that it did not mean anything to him. He shook my hand and shook

I had a field day passing out literature

the hand of Hector who stood a bit off to one side and did not intervene.

I had a sinking feeling that the letter from Noel was never going to make it to Julian's superiors. Somehow we had to communicate with them and with the entire FARC leadership. Little did I know that we would have to mobilize massive amounts of literature, solar radios, install new radio repeaters in at least two strategic locations (on *The Mountain* and three hundred miles north at the ABC triangle) and record key messages on cassettes and Cds and get them into the hands of the top leadership.

After our meeting with Noel, he went on a journey to seek his superiors in an attempt to help us. Unfortunately, before he reached them he walked right into an army ambush. Several of his men were killed, and Noel was seriously wounded in the side. He was out of commission for months in a remote guerrilla field hospital, where he was under orders to make no phone calls. I did not find this out until much later.

In Bogotá, General Reynaldo Castellano, commander of the entire Colombian Army, was very helpful. He offered to give me whatever support I needed. Sometimes I would meet with several generals in one day. Some of them, along with retired generals that I had known for years, attempted to help me face reality.

They told me not to blame myself for what had happened to Pacho. They also told me that the abduction of Pacho was probably one of the most difficult kidnappings to solve (some called it the most difficult kidnapping in the country to solve) because of who he was and because the guerrillas thought that he must have a lot of money.

Since I was kidnapped myself in 1983, I knew how it felt. It is a very difficult situation to face. With the kidnapping of my friend, Pacho, I found out how a kidnapping feels to the friends and family of the victim. It is even worse. No matter what the generals said, I definitely felt responsible for Pacho.

Literature and Galcom radios ready to be dropped by parachute into the guerrilla area

Finding myself in the eye of the hurricane I did know, however, beyond the shadow of a doubt that my conscience was clean. Whatever mistakes Pacho and I had made were done in good faith. I felt in my heart that the Lord would see us though.

New friendships strengthened and multiplied while some of those who had been our close friends and supporters began to shy away from us during this time of desperate need. Maybe they thought we would ask them for money to help pay a ransom. I began to find out who I could really count on.

Amazingly, it turned out that we had way more friends than I had ever imagined. Guerrillas began to come out of the woodwork trying to help us. Many paramilitary did the same. It was amazing the quality of the enlisted men and officers of the Colombian Armed Forces who did everything in their power to help us.

We quickly put together a short video about the situation with Pacho (Frank in English). Galcom used this to help provide us with thousands of solar powered fix-tuned radios. Voice of the Martyrs came to our aid with large amounts of Bibles and literature. People's Church of Toronto donated money for high mountain transmitters. The United Church of Los Alamos, NM helped. Gospel Center of Petersburgh, IN helped beef up our Short Wave transmitters. I could go on and on mentioning those who helped. Most importantly, thousands of people all over the world began to pray and intercede for us and for Frank.

This armoured personnel carrier helps
distribute our literature

REFUGE RADIO

PART VIII

PART VIII

Refuge Radio

CHAPTER 29

For years I had been longing to move our mountain radio repeater to a higher location. I had set my eye on a 5,600 ft. triangular peak which seemed to be in the center of much of the fighting. The army had a huge base on one side of the triangle. The paramilitary under Julian and then Ramiro were on the second side. The third side had guerrillas and then transitioned up into the higher reaches of *The Mountain* which ascended all the way up to 13,667 ft. within less than 10 miles. The guerrillas had been able to maintain control of this intermediate peak by mining the top and all points of access.

After the second meeting between Gabriel and Noel, I was given permission by all the powers that be to move my radio repeater (which up until now had been operating on a ridge at 4,200 ft. elevation) to the new site I like to call *El Tigre* (where one day I ran into a jaguar or Tigre as they are called in Colombia).

Our 500 ft radio tower at Lomalinda

The extra altitude would mean that the radio signal would extend for at least another 120 miles into the vast war zone. This would ensure excellent radio coverage to all the towns we had visited on our boat trip, and I knew that many top leaders of the Eastern Block of the FARC would now be well in range of our transmissions. In order to rescue Pacho, it was essential that their hearts be softened.

A few weeks before Pacho was taken, Alethia and I had decided to climb up to the top of *El Tigre* and scout around. We carefully found the only trail that seemed open and walked with great caution stepping only where there was a hard path, rock, hoof print or a boot print to help make sure that we didn't detonate a land mine.

When we finally got to the top, Alethia began to talk loudly to me in English. For some reason, a few guerrillas who had been hiding beside one of the ponds took off through the jungle like a herd of deer and never came back. The site was ideal for what we wanted.

The *campesinos* who had slowly been coming back to their abandoned farms on *The Mountain* were always friendly to us. Several of them got together to help me and my engineers build high tension power lines up to the top of *El Tigre* to power our transmitter. A wonderful fellow named "Aristotiles" returned to his farm and offered to look after our equipment.

As we blazed trail for the power lines and erected the steel towers to support them, people began to materialize from all over to help us. Cement, steel, gravel, transformers, voltage regulators, cable, and all kinds of radio equipment had to be carried by hand or hauled on mules up to the top. Some days there would be dozens of people helping us free of charge. Members of the establishments and even of the town council of a nearby town whose sympathies had been with the paramilitary now worked side by side with *campesinos* who had previously been run out of the area as suspected guerrilla sympathizers.

One day my son-in-law, Samuel Hernandez, asked a man in his early 50's named Anselmo, why he was helping us carry all this heavy equipment up the mountain. Anselmo, who was as strong as an ox, along with three other men, had put his shoulder to a pole tied to a 250 pound transformer.

Allan McGuirl and I beside the generator donated by Galcom

Several bullet scars in his side and extremities testified to a stint in his past; he had been the bodyguard of some very wealthy person. Anselmo and his friends were staggering up the side of *The Mountain* under the heavy load. Every couple hundred meters, another four men would spell them.

Anselmo said, "I am not an evangelical Christian, but I just know deep inside that this is the right thing to do".

After a while we hit a snag. Our crew kept running into mine fields, and we could find no one in the army, paramilitary, or guerrillas to

We found almost a dozen Bombs

deactivate them for us. We were able to dodge some of them but the area at the top of *El Tigre* where we needed to build the final set of electrical towers was heavily mined with 20 pound gas cylinders capable of destroying a 50 meter radius around each one. Remembering some previous advice from Noel, I decided that we would attempt to clear the mines ourselves.

Aristotiles and I took a long rope and carefully tied it to the ring on top of the first buried gas cylinder. Then we ran the rope over a bank as far away as possible and pulled on it with a whole bunch of guys. The gas cylinder came out of the ground and we were able to cut the wires to the detonator. Four mines came out uneventfully, but the fifth one blew up. After this, even though no one was hurt, none of the *campesinos* wanted to help us clear out anymore mines!

What we had done, however, was enough for us to be able to finish putting in the electrical power and install our transmitters. This site became operational a couple months after Pacho was taken.

Almost a year after our new mountain repeater was on the air, we discovered another gas cylinder less than 20 meters from the transmitter shed. We left it alone for another year and a half until a special Army engineering unit came by and was able to deactivate it. They located the trigger to the detonator of this powerful artifact less than a yard from the path that we had been using all this time to access the transmitter shed!

Deactivaded gas cylinders

CHAPTER 30

Late March, 2005

When it was clear that I was making no headway with Julian and the 28th front regarding the release of Pacho, the army began intense operations in the area to put pressure on the guerrillas. Thousands of men were deployed from at least three Brigades under the overall command of General Gilberto Rocha of the IV Division.

Tanks on wheels were sent in to take control of the roads. The Colombian Air Force had just upgraded their capability so that they could now place a bomb within 30 meters of the target instead of scattering the bombs all over. They now put the new technology to work in the ABC Triangle.

I tried to do everything in my power to make sure that they did not drop a bomb on Pacho. Many of the bombs seemed to be dropped on camps belonging to a second guerrilla group called the ELN. This began to produce tension between the FARC and the ELN. Helicopters began to place troops all around the rugged mountainous area where Pacho was being held. There were beautiful snow capped peaks in the background.

I began to search for a place to put a radio transmitter. Colonel Barrero, who had been second in command to General Saveedra a couple years before when the forward command post of the 7th Brigade had been at Lomalinda, now commanded the 16th Brigade in Yopal. He offered me the use of a huge Russian-built helicopter to fly all my equipment up to the top of a nearby mountain peak overlooking the entire area where he had some men. I was able to use their electrical power.

Alethia went with me, and we spent five days in semi-arctic conditions, installing the equipment at almost 13,000 ft. elevation. We had a hard time bouncing a signal up there from our studios located elsewhere. Finally we were able to rig a satellite link. We named this radio station *Garita Radio* (Refuge or Watchman Radio). Amazingly, a short time afterward, a Christian radio station in Duluth, Minnesota, started giving us some major help and became our sister station. The name of the station in Duluth was *Refuge Radio!*

The story about Pacho never made it into the secular news media, which was another major blessing. This would have greatly complicated his release because the expectations of the guerrillas would have been heightened. Well-meaning family and friends of his wanted to use the media to lay into the guerrillas. Fortunately, in the end they listened to me and gave me a free hand to deal with the problem.

I began to record special CDs explaining the situation for the top guerrilla commanders because I knew that Julian was not relaying any information to them that would be detrimental to himself. On Good Friday, I made a trip behind the Macarena mountains back to *La Julia* in the jurisdiction of the 40th front and left a letter and some of my CDs for the guerrilla commanders in that area. We now had radio coverage there as well, and I could tell that our radio messages were sinking in.

More time passed, and I was worn to a frazzle. Even so, I kept working on ways to get Bibles, solar powered Galcom radios fix-tuned to our frequencies and literature into the area where I knew they

A guerrilla girl receives
Rescue The Captors

were holding Pacho, as well as into all the areas where I suspected that the top guerrilla leadership might be located.

I did all this while trying to keep tabs on the massive land and air military operation in the ABC Triangle which at times involved up to 5000 men. I had to try to help make sure that someone did not inadvertently kill Pacho or cause the guerrillas to panic and kill him. As a spin off benefit, we had a field day evangelizing many of the troops.

Finally in July, things began to break. I got a message from the guerrillas, asking that if they were to release Pacho, would I help return the area to how it was before they captured him? In other words they wanted to know that if they released Pacho, would I help get all the military out of what they had always considered to be their area? I told them I would do what I could.

Wonder of wonders, I got a call from Noel and heard about how he had been shot right after our last meeting almost four months before. He told me he was back in his area but still a bit weak. He said that he had been doing everything possible to help solve our problem regarding Pacho.

Then, all of a sudden, the demands began to slide. I had refused to negotiate for money and Julian had continued to insist on 3.5 million dollars. Now all he wanted was 350 thousand. A week later he was down to 250 thousand. Then 200 thousand, then 150. Now, I knew for sure that the order had come from his superiors to solve the situation regarding Pacho.

A few weeks before, I had sent my last copy of the letter from Noel addressed to the 28th front to a guerrilla contact who had promised to give it to the right person. I had found out that the intense military operation had produced many casualties for the guerrillas; also, rumor had it that one of the angriest commanders, who had betrayed us, had become shell shocked after a bomb just missed him, so he left for Venezuela.

When the guerrilla demands hit 150 thousand dollars, a relative of Pacho wanted to go for it and pay. I said no. I not only wanted to get Pacho out. I wanted to make sure that he was happy when he got out. Since both of us had been life-long advocates of not paying any type of ransom that would incite kidnappers to keep on kidnapping people, I wanted to stay completely out of negotiations for money, and let Pacho handle it.

From the very beginning of his captivity, Pacho had told them that he would like to help them however he could, but that he could only afford to give them the Colombian equivalent of 70 thousand dollars. He stuck to his guns the whole time and never wavered. Finally, although it is against their policy of never dealing with the person they have kidnapped, this was the only offer available to them.

We have also found from experience that when dealing with situations like this in Colombia, two things are important: 1) Kidnappers must never make a profit or come out of a situation like this with incentive to do it again. 2) Once this is established, there must be some type of mechanism that allows them to "save face".

In other words, when they realize that they have made a big mistake, we must be careful not to rub it in. If we try to back them down too far without mercy, they may become unpredictable regarding the hostage. In this case Pacho was allowed to phone his brother and made arrangements to give them what he had promised.

On the way to pick up Pacho I was able to give literature and radios to people on all the different sides

CHAPTER 31

I went out to pick up Pacho on the day he was supposed to be released. The area was still in the midst of a huge military operation, and things got delayed for a day. The next day as I headed up into the mountains in my Toyota to where Pacho was to be released, a huge convoy of armored army vehicles came down the road headed right for us. There was no cell phone signal where I was at, so I asked the guerrilla contact man how I could make a phone call.

He pointed to a high almost vertical ridge, not far from the road, and said, "Come with me".

Somehow we made it up the sheer face, and, lo and behold, I had signal on my cell phone. I made a quick call to a Colonel and asked if he could stop the armored column and get them turned around and out of there.

After six months of roller coaster expectations, the Colonel still believed in me. The guerrilla contact man was amazed when a few minutes later the entire armored column turned around and left! Now we had another problem. We had climbed up such a steep cliff that I was almost unable to get back down. My new "friend" had to cut me a staff so that I could brace myself. When we got back to the Toyota I gave him a copy of *Rescue the Captors*, a Galcom radio and some great literature from Voice of the Martyrs.

I waited all day, and it started to get dark. Here I was in no man's land between guerrillas and possible paramilitary forces, and I had just sent the army packing! Should I leave? Should I stay? Even the lady who ran the little store near the end of the road was packing up to leave for town like she did every evening.

Obviously the area was not safe. I wondered if I should run the Toyota as far up the steep mountain road as I could and see if Pacho might be on his way down. There had been rain that morning which would cause all the streams to rise and delay things. Finally at dusk, word reached me that Pacho was, indeed, on his way.

I drove as fast as I could up the rough road. There came Pacho down the road, almost unrecognizable with long hair and a flowing white beard. After a big bear hug and a few tears we headed back down the road. As soon as we got into cell phone range, I began making calls on my two phones and handing the phones to Pacho. His friends and family reacted as if he had been resurrected from the dead!

The army asked if I could please bring Pacho to the military base at Yopal. I really stepped on it and by 9:30 PM we were there. Later Pacho told someone that I had been driving 100 miles per hour while making cell phone calls with both hands. I don't know how he could tell, because the speedometer has always been broke on my Toyota!

When President Alvaro Uribe took power, he made some major changes regarding the armed forces. No more partying on military bases. There was a war to be won. They were allowed one night a year of major festivities. This was on Army Day (kind of like Veterans Day).

Well, believe it or not, and unknown to me, the day Pacho was released was Army Day, and we drove into the biggest party you ever saw! There was an orchestra, a wonderful catered meal, everyone was in dress uniforms, there were all kinds of important invited guests, and the Colonel met us in the parking lot to usher us into the event.

We had no time to clean up or even change clothes. All of a sudden, we were sat down at the head table next to the Colonel. Pacho was chief guest

Issuing Bibles and Galcom Radios to the military

of honor. In the midst of all the hoopla and military gala, I kept ringing up Pacho's friends and family and passing him the phone until all my batteries went dead.

They all kept asking me what was going on because they had a hard time hearing over the phone due to the orchestra. I kept telling them, "Pacho is free, and we are having a party!"

Pacho was asked to give a keynote speech and he rose to the occasion giving heartfelt thanks to all the men who had risked their lives to put pressure on the guerrillas to help win his freedom. He also gave tribute to those who had given their lives in all the special military operations.

A few days later, I got a phone call from a very important person who was a cousin of Pacho. "How did you ever manage to convince those guerrillas to let him go? We thought that we would never see him again."

I responded, "God did a miracle! There is no other explanation."

Members of an elite unit receive books, Bibles and radios

Rescue the Captors II

MORE ANSWERED
PRAYERS

PART IX

PART IX

Many of the wounded have found the Lord

CHAPTER 32

A few weeks after the miraculous release of Francisco Vergara (Pacho), on August 7, 2005, Chaddy and I decided to fix up our river boat, *La Luz de la Verdad*, and send it down the Guaviare River towards Venezuela. Chaddy installed a motor while we touched up the paint and made new banners.

Four people volunteered as crew: Pedro, the captain, had been an orphan who Chaddy and I raised years before. He became very adept at running river launches and now, together with his wife, Aleida, who would be the cook, Pedro wanted to do something special for the Lord.

At the Lomalinda radio station, our station managers, Elsa and Celso Macias, were very keen about the river outreach. After prayer, Celso decided that the Lord wanted him on the crew in charge of the ministry. Clarisa, a Cuban lady who was in charge of our short wave radio signal called *The Voice of*

Allan McGuirl had a field day passing our his Galcom radios to all the fighting factions

Your Conscience, also felt a special call from God to go on this voyage.

We loaded the 70 ft. boat full of Bibles, literature and Galcom radios and gave them a big send off. At first, glowing reports came back but after a week there was total silence. Then we found out that although *La Luz de la Verdad* and crew had made it more than half way to Venezuela with great acceptance all along the way, guerrillas of the 44th front of the FARC had taken them hostage. No ransom demands were made. The guerrillas were mad about some literature that they found on board which knocked Marxism.

I had given strict orders that these hard hitting books not be on board our vessel while entering guerrilla territory. Somehow many boxes of *Marx and Satan* and *An Answer to the Atheists in Moscow* by Richard Wurmbrand were found by the guerrillas on our boat along with a lot of Galcom solar radios which also looked suspicious to them. Some guerrilla commanders were furious.

Right after the boat and crew were captured, samples of the literature and of the Galcom radios were sent with a guerrilla on a four wheeler deep into the jungle to the camp where the commanders lived. A few hours later, the Colombian Air Force dropped a bomb on the camp, killing almost everyone there.

The surviving guerrillas mistakenly suspected that the Galcom radio may have been carrying a homing device. This would have made us responsible for the bombing. It would take a miracle to save our crew. Now, instead of one person being held hostage, I was responsible for four who could be killed at any moment!

This man treasured his copy
of Rescue the Captors

CHAPTER 33

November, 2005

A civilian aircraft with four persons on board crashed into one of the upper ridges of *The Mountain*. Intense government air search and rescue missions failed to locate the downed Cessna 182 due to bad weather, coupled with the fact that the guerrillas had heavy machine guns in the area. On the ground Red Cross and Civil Defense rescue units attempted to reach the site of the crash but were turned back by the guerrillas.

Pacho, who enjoys search and rescue, asked me to fly with him in his airplane along with experts from the Civil Aeronautics who brought special equipment to help us locate the Emergency Locator Transmitter (ELT) of the crashed airplane, which was still active. After a briefing at the local Air Force Base we over flew the area and were able to obtain approximate coordinates of the crash site (which I marked on my GPS) even though it was difficult to see anything due to all the clouds.

The next day I was able to make contact with Noel, who authorized me to come up and search for the site of the accident as long as I came alone. I loaded the Toyota with food, equipment and supplies and headed for *The Mountain*. Noel met me himself, and we went up into the *páramo* which I had always wanted to see.

In the midst of these high alpine meadows nestled between jagged peaks, we found a beautiful lake at an altitude of 10,700 ft. which had been formed by glacial action during an ice age long ago. A crystal clear waterfall came over the edge of the terminal moraine which had formed the lake.

I realized this was a perfect place to put a water powered electric generator and power a radio repeater from on top of *The Mountain*. If I could get permission and finances to do this, we could have FM radio coverage all over south eastern Colombia and even into the border areas of neighboring countries.

For years, just about every time I had driven along the paved highway towards Lomalinda I would look up at *The Mountain* and claim it for the Lord. Now God had seen fit to let me actually set foot on the exact place that I needed. (We are still praying that permission will be granted by all the powers that be for us to use this site and that we will have the necessary resources.)

The airplane had crashed into the side of a steep 11,500 ft. ridge located a little over a mile from the lake. Everyone on board had been killed. I was able to speak with an Air Force general on the phone and outline the situation.

Then the Peruvian embassy called me because the pilot of the airplane was Peruvian and the general had told them that I was the only rescue person that had been able to get close to the site of the accident. They were able to give me the passenger list of those on board. With this I was able to prove to Noel and his comrades that this was a bona fide civilian airplane on a commercial air taxi flight and not some kind of government spy plane, as some of them suspected.

The guerrillas agreed to back off and let an Air Force helicopter land and remove the wreckage and bodies. This made everyone concerned happy. After I certified to the general that the area was clear and safe, an Air Force Blackhawk came in and took care of the situation as we watched from a prudent distance.

I spent my last day in the area at a cabin high on *The Mountain* where the guerrillas had a communications post. A beautiful girl with long black hair was the communications operator. She was nice, but strangely sad.

"Maria" switched stations

For a few minutes the next morning everyone else left, and I was alone with her. She told me that she had read my book twice and that she

The men enjoy reading their Bibles

liked to listen to my radio station. I asked her which one? The station from Lomalinda or the one I repeat from *El Tigre*?

She said, "I am from *El Tigre*."

Then I mentioned a *campesino* from that area who was a very good friend of mine and "Maria" broke into tears. Almost in a whisper, she said, "He is my father".

Her family had been one of the first to receive the Gospel on *The Mountain*. A red Galcom radio was on the porch of their house the first time I met them years before. They had been praying to be able to meet the person that was speaking on the radio, and the Lord led me to them. For years they had been asking me to search for their oldest daughter who had rebelled, left home and was eventually taken away by the guerrillas. They had not seen her since.

I pulled out my camera, which I almost never carry on delicate trips, and was able to get a picture of her. After a bit of reflection and noticing the crutches beside the door, I finally realized that Maria was missing her left foot. I later learned that she had stepped on a mine. Even though I tried, there was nothing more I could do at the time to get her out of there, so I gave her the phone number of her father and I took the picture to her mother.

I was able to have a good talk with Noel and Eduardo and thank them for helping to extricate Pacho from such a difficult situation. They were glad that I had been able to come and visit them. Then I told them about my river boat crew. They promised to do everything in their power to help us.

Later I found out that many other guerrillas had also been calling the 44th front to put in a good word for us. One of the commanders of the group that held Pacho reportedly called them up and said, "We enjoyed the books, Bibles and radios. They were a great blessing to us!"

A few days after I came back from *The Mountain,* our river boat crew was released unharmed. They had spent 49 days in captivity. But the guerrillas are still holding the boat as I write this in November of 2007. From time to time, as they read all the different literature left on board the boat, some of them continue to fulminate against us. One said that if he had read the books, earlier he would have never let our crew return alive.

CHAPTER 34

December, 2005

Hector Gonzalez got a call from our friend, Diego Montoya Molina. Diego wanted to know if I wanted his sport category airplane. The plane was worth over 50 thousand dollars, but he had been offering it to me for 40 thousand. Now, Diego and his wife, Amparo (who had been listening to our radio programs for twenty years) wanted to help our ministry. They could sell us the airplane for 17 thousand!

I did not have the money, but I was able to present this deal to some friends from Voice of the Martyrs (VOM) who were visiting us. The project was almost instantly approved and they even gave us some money for taxes, licenses, maintenance and operating expenses. With the help and gifts of many others, we began to drop Bibles, books and Galcom radios by parachute into areas too difficult to reach by any other means.

Twenty years had gone by since we had sold

A soldier receives a "Truth Pack" with parachute at night

our last missionary airplane. For the past ten years, there had been no missionary aircraft at all in Colombia due to all the violence and unrest. Now we were back in the air!

VOM was planning to dedicate the February, 2006 issue of their magazine in the USA to report on Colombia. I told them about Maria and sent them her picture. They wrote a column about her titled "Searching for Maria." I was asked if they should block out her eyes in the picture for security concerns. But if people could see the look in her eyes I felt they would be much more inclined to pray for her. The picture was published as is, and the magazine went out to several hundred thousand households.

I spent the next several months flying the airplane over places that were difficult or impossible to reach on the ground. Most everyone was very receptive to the packages, which we call "Truth Packs" that I was dropping by parachute. The packages contained a Bible, a Galcom solar radio and several good books. In the more secure areas, I could fly at tree top level and drop the parachutes with great precision almost into the hands of the expectant people.

In other places the guerrillas would shoot at me. If I was flying low with the window open, I could hear the muzzle blast from the weapons. When flying a bit higher all I could hear was a super-sonic blip from each bullet that came near the airplane. I am sure that they must have fired hundreds and hundreds (maybe even thousands) of bullets at me, but by the grace of God they only hit me once. On the other hand, I am confident that I have placed the vast majority of our "Truth Packs" right on target!

My father and I
with the airplane

CHAPTER 35

July, 2006

I received a call from someone to the south of *The Mountain* that claimed to be a friend of Noel. It was difficult for me to recognize the voice over the phone, but it did seem vaguely familiar. The voice said that Colombian Army forces had been driving them south down the eastern range of the Andes. The guerrillas had fled up into the mountains leaving behind some *campesinos* that they feared might be murdered by the paramilitary. The voice wanted to know if I could come out and take these people to a safe place.

It was a very difficult place to get to. First I had to pass through a known haven for common thieves and bandits on the edge of a huge drug-growing area, which had just been sprayed with herbicide by a US funded initiative to eradicate drugs. The immediate effect of this was that lots of people accustomed to easy money were now desperately looking for someone to rob or kidnap.

Then there were rogue paramilitary units scattered here and there that sometimes even fought against one another. There were also other guerrilla units in the area, some of which were not very friendly towards me (as evidenced by the number of shots they had recently fired at the airplane). All this in addition to the normal army and police units who can have varying degrees of corruption or even ties to illegal armed groups. However, for a long time now, I have been finding more and more strong Christians within the Colombian Armed Forces.

As on many other occasions, I had to make a snap decision over the phone. This could easily be some kind of trap or set up. I tried to delay to see if I could somehow check this out with other, more t r u s t e d sources.

T h e voice was insistent. If these people were to be saved, I must go immediately. I said yes, hung up the phone and

Many of these men have turned to the Lord

phone and took off at 3 AM in the Toyota. I managed to get through the complicated and very active war zone, making it through the bandit-infested area under cover of darkness (I have found that bandits don't ever seem to get up very early, although the guerrillas do).

Guerrillas love our radios

At a small port on the edge of the jungle at the base of the mountains, I found the people I was looking for. I had to make two round trips, and on my second journey, I hit the jackpot when "Maria" stepped out of a semi abandoned general store with a big grin on her face.

When the army attacked the guerrilla unit, she was unable to flee with her comrades due to her clumsy wooden leg. She hid by herself in the thick jungle for several days, and then a friend helped her make it down a very difficult trail to the road. It was then they had called me. I took her to our Lomalinda radio station, entrusted her to our station manager, Elsa, and left to take care of other pressing concerns.

Unknown to me, in addition to her communications duties, "Maria" had been one of the anchor radio announcers on the guerrilla radio station, *The Voice of the Resistance*. Now, reveling in her new found freedom and anxious to please, she pitched in and offered to help Elsa and the others on our FM station. Soon she was happily reading news and announcements as well as filling in for the occasional DJ who was sick or on leave.

Noel had always told me, "Listen to our radio station, and I will listen to yours. Let's critique one another."

If I had paid more attention to him, I would have been able to foresee what was coming. In a huge sector of the eastern war zone, many people only listened to two radio stations: ours or the guerrillas. Everyone could easily recognize the voice of all their favorite announcers. When "Maria" abruptly changed stations, it was like what would have happened if someone like Tokyo Rose had changed stations in WWII!

When the guerrillas had taken our two radio station managers, Celso and Clarisa, hostage for 49 days, everyone in the area had known of it even though we kept things very low key over the air. Many people felt sorry for us and thought that we had been greatly humiliated by the guerrillas of the 44th front.

Truth Packs ready for deployment. Men and women from all sides have been helping us including the Colombian Air Force

Now it was the other way around. In the eyes of the greater community, we had made a tremendous comeback and the tables were turned. The situation started to get danger-ous, however, because some of the guerrilla leader-ship wanted "Maria" back immediately.

Needless to say, our listener ratings shot sky high as everyone tuned in and could not believe what they were hearing. I tried to explain to the guerril-las that we could not force "Maria" to go back to them, because her parents and family had now heard her over the air, and she had been reunited with them.

I decided not to rub it in too bad because they might become unpredictable; so I left "Maria" on the air for a few more days and then sent her to the hospital to have her leg properly looked after. VOM and many other gracious people helped with her surgery and new artificial limb. Truly the Lord an-swered many prayers.

Many hunger and thrist for righteousness

WITH WINGS AS AN EAGLE

PART X

PART X

Converted former guerrillas prepare *Truth Packs* to be deployed with parachutes

CHAPTER 36

Fall, 2006

I do not have a sharp recollection of all the details of the fall of 2006 due the volume and magnitude of the activity. Early morning trips up the different mountains to keep our various repeaters functioning blend together with strenuous trips back into the mountains, jungles and rivers to share with guerrillas or with paramilitary or whoever the Lord brought me into contact with. (We also continue to go over numerous financial hurdles as expenses mount to keep all the radio stations on the air.)

Years ago I had to give up my habit of ministering in the North during the winter months. For the past seven years, I have felt it is better to be found at my post in Colombia, always ready to pick up on any opportunity. Sometimes I have prayed for someone for ten or fifteen or more years and then have to make a quick decision based on one phone call that may never be repeated.

Lots of ministries can travel and speak in North America, but there are few available to minister to the fighting factions of Colombia. The Lord has multiplied our efforts through radio and literature, but personal contact is essential.

"How will you stay afloat financially if you never take a furlough to touch base with your supporters?" I am constantly asked.

The only answer to that is that although we have continually gone through times of great need, the Lord has never let us down. The bottom line for us is that if we concentrate on doing things God's way, He will provide what we need. He always has.

It also has been a very profitable use of our time to attend certain Conventions such as Mission's Fest held the last week in January in Vancouver. We go every year or two.

Noel once asked me how I could preach so many different messages over the radio. On his station everything is carefully scripted and read. No one can easily understand the grace that God has granted me and to those with me, to simply be able to open our Bibles to any chapter

The fields are ripe unto harvest ...

and preach. The majority of my messages go verse by verse through the Bible, a chapter per message.

When our volunteers (many of them are top-notch lawyers, doctors or university professors) come

A sentinel reads Rescue the Captors. Note bullet holes in window

into the studio to record radio programs, at first, most of them used to ask me how to prepare for the programs. I always tell them to prepare their hearts. Effective ministry must flow from the heart if it is to really change those who are hard and bitter.

In the Bible many kings of Israel and Judah failed because they did not prepare their hearts to follow God. Solomon with all his wisdom did not follow the simple advice of his father, David, who said, "Young man, above all else, Guard thy heart." The result was disaster.

It is greatly encouraging to travel through what used to be pristine wilderness, now ravaged by war and the drug industry, and find those whose hearts have been softened by the direct dealings of God. The missionaries, pastors and evangelists who were forced to flee, or who were sent home by their international mission organizations are being replaced

These policemen gave us a hearty welcome

by those who *used to be* guerrillas, paramilitary or drug traffickers!

Years ago, I sent some copies of *Marx and Satan,* the hard hitting book by Richard Wurmbrand, with a young volunteer from a local church near our radio station who wanted to evangelize guerrillas. There was a nice picture of Karl Marx on the cover and the young man (I can remember his face but not his name) ran into a group of paramilitary on his way to find the guerrillas.

The paramilitary took one look at the picture of Marx and shot him dead, thinking he was taking Marxist literature to the guerrillas. Then, after killing the missionary, they began to read the books they found in his back pack. One of them was soundly converted, left the paramilitary organization, and is pastoring an effective local church today.

There are scores of unsung, nameless heroes scattered across the battleground of Colombia. Virtually anyone who turns to the Lord will immediately begin to suffer some form of persecution, no matter what group or side they belong to.

But we have a tremendous opportunity before

us. Even though there are vast areas where most of the religious groups have been silenced. The church buildings have been destroyed or converted into community centers. Professional pastors and clergy have been banished.

In some places like those controlled by the 44th front, all evangelical meetings of any kind have been banned for over 20 years. But in the midst of this no one has been able to stop an individual from having personal and intimate contact with God. True Christians are multiplying like rabbits.

True Christianity has always done well under persecution. It is material prosperity and apparent safety that throughout history has been the bane of the people of God.

With the support of the commanding general, Bibles and Galcom radios have been issued to all the troops

CHAPTER 37

Deuteronomy 2:25:

"This day I will begin to put the fear of thee and the dread of thee upon the peoples that are under the full heaven who shall hear the report of thee and shall tremble and be in anguish because of thee."

The same theme is woven through the Song of Solomon when the Shulamite comes forth out of the wilderness leaning on her beloved and all of a sudden there is a fear and an awe regarding her. There is a certain aroma about her because of her being with Him. And there has been a tremendous change. (See Song 3:6; 6:10; 8:5)

All of us know what it means to have to run from the enemy. We have all been in situations where we have had to run. But the Lord is now bringing about a change. Years ago I knew the Lord had called me to evangelize and rescue guerrillas. When I was ransomed and rescued from the guerrilla camp, my heart went out to my captors because, I thought, "Who is concerned about getting them out of there?" Many of them started out with apparent good intentions and then got trapped in a horrendous situation.

As things got worse in Colombia, I can remember sitting in Bogotá, wondering how to get out into the rural areas. I would pray for days and then make a break for it to see if we could get out to where we needed to go and then praise the Lord that we didn't run into any guerrillas (who were kidnapping people at random and planting explosives on most of the roads).

Then, after a while the Lord started to change things. Not that we would go off and be reckless, but I began to detect signs that there were guerrillas out there that were way more afraid of me than I was of them.

I began to sense that under the surface some of these guys that seemed so tough and ruthless were scared to death that God was going to get a hold of them. I would send books out to the guerrilla leadership first and then send word that I would like to go out and see them. But they would disappear; some of them didn't want to see me for anything. This was because the Lord started to turn the situation around.

It's dangerous to claim victory too soon. So I certainly don't want to give you folks the impression that everything is won. But we're seeing some changes, and they are exciting changes. There are details from time to time that really, really encourage us.

In 2005, I had to deal with several hostage situations, and by the grace of God, we were able to get our people back. But this year, things have turned around, and we have been able, in the name of the Lord, to take some/of them "hostage". Over the years, from time to time, we have had to deal with them; now they also have to deal with us.

We obtained this little airplane after having not had an airplane for over twenty years. There have not been any missionary airplanes in Colombia for over ten years. It's like this whole area of flying, symbolically for me, has been kind of like coming into a higher realm.

In the book of Revelation, there is a "woman" (representing an overcoming Church) who has to flee to the wilderness with a "dragon" after her. But after a while she learns, and God gives her wings like those of an eagle. She gets to fly over all the trouble, and the dragon that was after her has lost his position in the heavenly realm. He gets cast out of heaven unto the earth. Then he gets really upset because he realizes he doesn't have much time and now he can't fly anymore. Now she has the "wings" instead of him! (See Revelation Chapter 12).

And if you continue to Revelation Chapter 20, God is going to send an angel with a chain and lock him up in the bottomless pit for a thousand years. So now the Devil is in trouble, and he is headed for even worse trouble. He is about to be cast down unto the earth. But he is still very dangerous to those that are in his realm. In Job it talks about him being chained in darkness, but if you shy away from the truth and insist on remaining in the realm of darkness and get inside the reach of his chain, it can be very serious.

If we stay in the light, close to the Lord, anything the Devil tries will backfire against him in the end. All things work together for good for those who love the Lord and are called according to His purpose, the Lord's purpose. So if it's really the Lord's purpose, if we've really been called by Him, if we've really been sent by Him to do what we're doing, then no matter what the Devil does, it just plays into God's hands.

However, if we are out there doing something that *we* thought was a good idea; the Devil will have us for lunch. Many Christian missionaries that wanted to do "good" things have been run out of eastern Colombia.

Much of eastern Colombia has become a spiritual void, a spiritual black hole. So we have been beaming radio messages into the areas controlled by the various violent groups with a number of different transmission systems and following up with literature, and then, if God opens the door, we can make personal visits. In some places where Christian meetings have been banned for years, I estimate that up to half the population has turned to the Lord.

Here I am with my son, Russell Jr. This Cessna 180 was recently donated to us

CHAPTER 38

December, 2006

On several occasions, we have unintentionally flown directly over the guerrillas. I had one incident happen four days ago, when I was near the end of my flight, and I decided to fly over one last house. This little airplane turns on a dime, so I fly really low and find all these houses and drop them all a package on their doorstep. Many of the people that live in these areas are not allowed to leave. The guerrillas are using them as human shields to stop the government advance.

The government is out spraying the drug fields that almost everybody lives off of with herbicide. This causes their former prosperity to vanish. When their drug field gets sprayed, their pasture gets sprayed, their garden gets sprayed, everything gets sprayed, and it all dries up. On top of this, there are all these armed people running around trying to steal from them. It is a big mess, but it is a perfect time for all of them to turn to the Lord.

So we are dropping "Truth Packs" with New Testaments and books and solar-powered radios locked on to our frequencies. But when I came over this last house, it had some guerrillas inside. They couldn't hear the plane, because it doesn't sound very loud until we are right on top of them.

When they finally realized the airplane was going to go right over the top of the house, (about 150 ft. above the house), they all started running for their lives. They weren't trying to shoot at the plane, they were just trying to save themselves and get out of there and into the jungle. I saw one jumping over the banister and out over the side of the porch, thinking that a bomb was going to fall on top of him.

As I let the parachute drop right over their heads, I thought, "You know, the Lord really turned this thing around, I used to be so scared of those guys, and now the Lord is putting the fear and dread of me into them!"

And so, as we come closer into the day that the Lord has for us here, we can expect the tables to turn.

A parachute with a Galcom radio falls onto ground covered with spent rifle cartridges

All of the enemies that we had thought were impossible, all these giants, this humanistic system that

Alan McGuirl of Galcom gives a radio to a lady in guerrilla territory who has come to know the Lord

surrounds us, all of the religious entities that have become corrupt and seemingly so powerful and have absorbed the resources from what should really be God's people and have spent it on themselves or on fruitless endeavors, that they think is evangelism, (but a lot of it is more like when the Scripture mentions the Pharisees traveling over land and sea to make one proselyte, and when they get done with him, they made him twice the son of the Devil than they themselves are). All of this is going to begin to retreat, crumble and come to an end. (See Matthew Chapter 23).

Because those with false hearts, like tares that are planted in among the wheat, the Scripture says that they are the sons of the evil one. They act like the sons of light, but their light is the light of this world, and it isn't the real light. Jesus said that first the tares would be gathered together into bundles and burned, and then the wheat would be harvested and stored in His barn. (See Matthew Chapter 13).

When those who are supposed to be God's people turn from God and go after their own understanding and seek man's light instead of God's light, the end of the matter isn't just darkness and deception. They actually begin to think that the darkness that they now have is light, and they think that the real light that the real people of God have is darkness. They believe that sweet is sour and that sour is sweet, and they lose all perspective. They do not believe that the warnings in Scripture apply to them.

In the Sermon of the Mount, in Matthew Chapter 7, Jesus says that if the light that is in us is really darkness, then what is *real* darkness going to be like? He says that our eye must be single. Our eye is what perceives the light, and unless we have an eye only to look to Him, we are not only going to lose track of the light, we are going to end up after something else that we think is the light, and then the real light will not make sense to us anymore. This is why those who won't receive the truth are given over to a strong delusion. (See 2 Thessalonians 2:10,11).

The first arena I believe that God is going to deal with as we come into the Day of the Lord is the religious realm in which people are

Distribution of Bibles and radios to elite units including the Presidential Guard

seriously misrepresenting God. But I think that the dealings of God will soon affect all the places from which we have had to run and all the things that we have feared that are not the fear of the Lord. The Lord is in the process of dealing with all of this in the lives of those who will embrace the Truth ahead of time. It gives us this tremendous, tremendous identity in Christ and a whole new perspective in which to operate.

Massive Bible and radio distribution to tens of thousands of men

TOWARD A PERFECT HEART

PART XI

PART XI

My daughter, Lisa, (now Age 25) and my
Son-in-law, Sammy, work with us full time

CHAPTER 39

1 Corinthians 1:21

"For in the wisdom of God, since the world by wisdom knew not God, It pleased God by the foolishness of preaching to save those that believe."

Through all the years that I have been in radio ministry, I've never been able to preach very well over the radio just into a cold microphone in the studio. So, for the preaching that we put out over the radio, we always have a meeting and invite people to come. It's a very interesting thing because depending on who comes, it has a big impact on the message. Sometimes I have to go back over my messages and listen to them three of four times to learn whatever it was that the Lord drew out of me when certain people were present.

Once when I was in the middle of a series on the Gospel of John and was planning on preaching on John Chapter 17, one of the main guerrilla leaders walked into the meeting and sat down. I ended up with a totally different message, but it still tied in with John 17!

One of the first areas where the Scripture dwells on perfection has to do with the heart. The Scripture speaks of men that had a perfect heart toward the Lord. What that word, *perfect* means is that they had a heart for God, and not for themselves. It's that simple! And really what God is after is to place His heart in us, and His heart is perfect. So it's not a situation of trying to correct and improve and somehow rehabilitate Adam, Adam's life, and what we've received from Adam.

Even though while we are in the life that we received from Adam, God can give us natural and spiritual gifts; unless we come under the direct dealings of the Holy Spirit of God, we can't get out from under Adam's life and into Christ's life. The only one who can do that for us is the Spirit of God. This is what water baptism symbolizes.

Dropping a Truth Pack

God wants to come and begin a work in us, if we will allow him to come in. If He has His way and if He finishes the work that He wants to begin in each and every one of us, what Scripture calls the *old man* in us will die, and Jesus Christ will be alive in us, not just in theory, but proven in the practice of the circumstances of everyday life. The apostle

Paul said that this was happening in his life on a daily basis.

Here in Colombia there has been a lot of persecution of Christians and other problems. But my brother Chaddy has always said that it is easier to live for the Lord in the middle of this war zone in Colombia, because we haven't got any other choice. If we don't depend on the Lord, someone may shoot us or do something really nasty to us. The hardest

Allan McGuirl of Galcom inspects our radio tower at Lomalinda

place I can think of to live for God is in prosperous, complacent, tranquil North America.

This has been the problem that has caused the most damage for God's people throughout history. All the way through the Old Testament, into the New Testament, and throughout the Church Age, God's people have not done very well under prosperity. What seems like peace is deceptive, because what seems like peace in this world is really only false peace, designed to lure us to sleep. The true peace from the Lord comes when our lives are under the control of the Holy Spirit.

It takes the Holy Spirit to come on the scene with His truth. When He applies the truth, that's when we end up in peace. God's peace doesn't really have anything to do with the circumstances around us. We can be in peace inside under the leadership and guidance of the Holy Spirit of God, as long as we want the truth, and as long as we're willing to let Him apply the truth to our lives.

It's very interesting that the word, *truth*, and the word, *peace*, are each used in roughly 350 verses of the Bible. And there are 12 verses in the Scripture in which truth and peace occur in the same verse. Twelve is a number that has to do with divine order, with God's order. If we won't let Him line us up with the Truth, we will never be at peace.

Here I am with Ray Rising and Russell Jr. on the day of his release 10 years ago. Ray is now our next door neighbor and is always willing to help with radio ministry

CHAPTER 40

God tried to apply the truth to the life of Cain at the beginning of the book of Genesis. He told him what he needed to do. God told Cain that sin was at the door if Cain were to continue in the attitude that he had. And after Cain murdered his brother, the sentence that God placed on the life of Cain was that he was going to wander to and fro and he would never be at peace.

God did not give Cain an immediate death sentence. He let Cain live out the rest of his life in unrest, hoping he would turn back to God and find repentance. And so it is for all who follow the footsteps of Cain.

Cain attempted to present the work of his hands to the Lord. He worked hard in the field, harvested grain, and came and offered it to the Lord. But the Lord not only would not receive the present that Cain offered, He would not receive Cain. The word for Cain's offering, which in the Jubilee Bible is translated as "present," goes all the way through the Scripture, all through the Old Testament and into the New Testament. This word represents the work of our hands. Our own work is not acceptable to God. We must be under a blood covenant. Scripture says that, "The life is in the blood." What we do in our own life can never please God or cause Him to accept us.

The moral of the story is that we must be under a blood covenant with God like Abel. Abel simply came and offered a lamb, and by that recognized that he wasn't going to be able to please God or to be acceptable unto God in His own life. The sacrifice of Abel demonstrated that it was going to take another life, the life of Jesus Christ, the Lamb of God, who would shed his blood for us later on. Abel was looking forward by faith to the sacrifice of Jesus, and God received him.

When we are covered by the blood of Jesus, God begins to work in and through us by the Holy Spirit. This work *is* acceptable to God. Throughout the Old Testament, the "grain offering" or "present" had to be offered together with a blood sacrifice in order for God to approve.

Cain got all bent out of shape because he thought he had worked harder than his brother. He did all this hard work, and God would not receive him. He got so mad about it that he killed his brother. The same situation is still going on and is being repeated over and over. Two types of seed, representing two distinct spiritual generations, have been in conflict since the beginning of history.

The Devil has always been trying to snuff out the Godly generation, but the Devil did not know what God's plan was. The Scripture is clear;

I contemplate the natural beauty of Colombia from The Mountain

it says that if the princes of this world would have known, they would have never crucified the Lord of glory. Jesus came, and not only did He break the power of sin and death, but He opened the way for us to get back into the presence of the Father.

Not in our old corrupt life, but in His clean and perfect life. Not just so that we could get back to the presence of the Father and be like Adam before the fall, but so that the works of our hands would be acceptable again unto God, because the work would not be done in the corruption of our life; it would be done in His life. And so throughout the Law of Moses, when anyone went to offer a blood sacrifice, it was linked to what the King James Bible calls a "grain offering" and that is the same word that in the beginning is translated, "present".

This is what Cain tried to offer, and what God rejected. But God will receive us and the work done in and through us by the Holy Spirit, if we are in a blood covenant with Him.

CHAPTER 41

As I was working on the translation of the Jubilee 2000 Bible out of the old Spanish, I came to a place where I couldn't proceed anymore. It was a rather strange place in the Bible to get hung up. I got stuck for about six months in between the end of the book of Exodus and the first seven chapters or so of the book of Leviticus.

I had gone through the New Testament, I had gone through the Prophets, I had gone through the Psalms, I had thoroughly studied a lot of terminology and background, and now I was coming up through the beginning of the books of Moses. The Lord had been putting His hand and anointing on the translation, and I could tell at the end of each verse when it was how the Lord wanted it. All of a sudden, I got hung up and could not move on because I no longer could sense the approval of the Lord on what I was doing.

I began to slowly discover problems concerning terminology and also regarding extra words which had been inserted. Normally, when the translators from the Reformation would for proper grammar or clarity of meaning insert a word into the translation of the Scriptures that was not in the Original, it would be put in italics so that you could tell. We have continued that tradition in the Jubilee Bible, but here in Leviticus, I found a number of words added that were not in italics, and that was part of the problem.

In the first few chapters of Leviticus, a "sin offering" is introduced and then a "guilt offering". It turns out that in the original, it does not say *offering*. It's not talking about offering a bullock or a calf as a "sin offering", the Original says that the sinner was to place his or her hands on the animal, and it would symbolically become the sin.

God is not interested in our giving Him an *offering* so that we can keep on sinning; He wants us to offer the sin, so that we can help Him slit the throat on that sin, and bleed it to death. Then He wants to apply the fire of God on the altar of God and convert our "sin" into a pile of inert ashes. This is God's plan to deliver us from the power of sin. Jesus became sin for us, so that we might become the righteousness of God.

Adam and Eve didn't get into trouble just over the knowledge of evil; it was the knowledge of *good* and evil. That which is not of faith is sin. So if we're doing something that we think is good and wonderful, and if it isn't of faith; if it doesn't have to do with a relationship and dependence on God and on the life of Jesus Christ, it is sin. This is where many well-meaning Christian people have gotten hung up over the years.

Most of the photos in this book were taken by my daughter, Alethia. Here she is crossing a bridge into guerrilla territory

We work on our vocabulary, and we work on certain areas of our behavior. Because we're not drunk, or we're not in some type of sexual immorality, and we're not telling lies, and we're talking like Christians, we think that now we are righteous people. This is the same problem that the Jews got into. They got into a situation that the Bible describes as our own righteousness, which is as filthy rags before the Lord. So when we think that we are doing something wonderful, and when our work is not linked to God's life, we're basically back in the same problem as Cain.

Cain worked so hard and got what he thought was a wonderful crop and came and offered it to God, and did not get accepted. Cain really got upset over the matter when his brother who wasn't out there sweating in the field, took a little lamb and offered it to God and was accepted.

Since Cain killed his brother Abel, we have had all kinds of tragic stories throughout the years. People have thought they were doing God a favor when they went out and killed someone who was actually operating in the name and in the nature and life of Jesus Christ. This spirit of the Inquisition is even now alive and well in Christendom, except that instead of physical violence, many now resort to killing the reputation of those who have truly been accepted by God.

What we think it is and what it appears to be in terms of our own natural way of thinking isn't even close to God's way of thinking. And so from the very beginning, God told them to offer their sin and that sin had "horns", it had "hoofs," and it could get really nasty. If you were not careful, that "sin" could kick you, it could trample you, it could gore you. It took the help of a "priest" or a "Levite" to get the "sin" tied and on the altar and its throat slit, and to apply the fire of God to the whole mess.

The book of Leviticus goes on to tell how the inward parts have to be run through the fire and all kinds of instructions that seem like meaningless rigmarole, but it is full of important and very symbolic details about how God wants to deal with sin in our lives.

The New Testament says that the Lord Jesus is now the *only* mediator between us and God.

Giving a Galcom solar radio to one of my little friends

Jesus is our new high priest, seated at the right hand of the Father with *all* power and authority to bring us into compliance with the New Covenant.

The Scripture also says that we are to "confess our sins one to another" and bring them out into the light so that Jesus can apply the fire of the Holy Spirit and thoroughly cleanse us. God does not want us to offer Him something instead of our sin. He wants us to bring our sin into the light and allow Him to help us put an end to it.

And then the next sacrifice isn't a guilt *offering*, *it's the actual guilt that he wants to do away with!* He wants to repeat the process for putting an end to our sin with a "he goat" that represents our guilt. Those he goats are nasty; if you turn your back on them, they can really let you have it.

A lot of people get hung up trying to enter the Kingdom of God and never really become productive; they never produce the fruit of the Spirit because their guilt never gets killed on the altar of God. They are always hung up over something out of the past, and the enemy, who is also called the accuser of the brethren, will take that guilt and continue to rake them over the coals. It can be something they did or something that someone else did to them that continues to rob them of peace and victory.

Not only that, but false religion feeds on this. One of the things that makes it run is guilt. Man-made religion sets up things that are impossible for the people to do. Then when they can't do them and when they feel guilty, they have to keep coming back to these, what the Scripture calls, blind guides. They continue to manipulate the situation and "absolve" the people, but they never kill the guilt.

False church and false religion never deliver the people from sin and guilt. They teach the people that they connot avoid sinning in word, thought, deed and by omission on a daily basis. They teach that the only way to absolve sin and to not feel guilty is to do what their church leadership says. So they have endless religious meetings and procedures.

In the midst of all this, they come up with all kinds of plans and programs that God does not bless. It is true that we are all sinners who have fallen short of the glory of God, but Jesus Christ is not a sinner, and He wants to live inside of us and take charge of our lives.

Off on another adventure . . .

CHAPTER 42

Now, amazingly enough, after Scripture clearly states that salvation is of faith and by grace, when we get to where the Bible mentions judgment, God says that each one is going to be judged by their works. Our own "good" works won't save us; it has to be God's work in us and through us.

Jesus said that in the end it was going to be like the sheep and the goats. He is going to separate them out. The "goats" are not going to enter in to what He has for those who are genuinely His.

And when it comes down to why, He will say, "I was hungry, I was thirsty, I was naked, I was in prison, and you didn't attend to Me."

And they will say, "But Lord, we never saw you like that; we never turned our back on you."

And He will say, "When you did it unto the least of one of these that are really mine, when you turned your back on one of them, you turned your back on Me."

And the ones that enter into the kingdom, when He tells them why, they won't seem to realize what they had been doing either. But you see, they hadn't just been doing "good" works, they had been doing what He wanted.

When His life is in us, we are able to witness to what He wants, and where He wants us, and we don't miss with our effort. When His life is in us, our pleasure is to please Him, and we do it naturally because our heart, soul, mind and goals have been transformed.

Consider when Jesus dealt with the rich young ruler. We don't know where the rich young ruler got his money, but it was holding him up. He was trusting in that money and in those possessions.

Jesus didn't tell him, "Well, if you really want to come on board with the Jesus of Nazareth Crusade, go over and see Judas, he's our treasurer. Give Judas all your money, and he'll put it in the bag."

He didn't say that at

Orphan children who have taken refuge in an abandoned church building. They are fortunate if they get one good meal a day. Rural Colombia is filled with widows and orphans

Orphans receive CARE packs from VOM which include the Gospel

all to him. He said, "Go and give it to the poor and *you* come and follow me."

Jesus was not primarily after the money at all, He was after the young man. Jesus loved him, Jesus wanted him. But if there is anything else in our life that has a higher priority than the Lord, it has to be dealt with, or we can't follow the Lord properly.

And so the Lord did a number of things that don't look right according to our priorities, but they are according to His priorities. He went over to Zacheus's place and Zacheus had a nasty reputation all over town.

Jesus called him down out of a tree and told him, "I'm going to have lunch at your place."

The Lord didn't really even tell Zacheus what to do. As the Lord was there having a meal all of a sudden Zacheus came under conviction.

He started saying, "You know, if I've wronged anybody, I'm going to pay it back four-fold and I'm going to take half of what I have and I'm going to give it to the poor."

And the Lord didn't say, "Well, I was just thinking about the rich, young, ruler, and I told him to give up everything,"

He didn't say that at all. He just said, "Today, salvation has come to this household." Each case was totally different.

Matthew, the tax-collector, left everything and followed the Lord. The Scripture says that the Lord is no respecter of persons, yet He reserves the right to handle each and every case however He wants to do it.

Another thing that really tends to bind us up is that from time to time someone will have a genuine experience with the Lord, and a tremendous transformation will take place in their life, but then the temptation is to try to build a spiritual assembly line and try to get everybody else to jump through the same hoops, and that's not the way God does things.

I mean, there are certain things about Him that don't change, and there are certain standards that He has that He won't bend, but He takes a unique ap-

In many villages up to one third of the children are orphans. There are also many elderly who have no one left to care for them

proach to everybody and to each and every situation.

If you look through the Old Testament, in all of the battles that King David won, the patterns all changed. In one it was to send the young people first, and the key to the whole thing was not in learning a certain set of procedures about how to overcome the enemy.

The key to the whole thing was that David had to hear from God under each new set of circumstances. Unless he heard from God, they would not be able to win the victory. The key of David's success was hearing from God and doing what God said. "Should I go, or should I not go? Should I pursue them? What should I do, Lord?"

After fighting prolonged battles with fear and uncertainty, I have been thrilled to hear time and time again the clear voice of the Lord in my spirit telling me to go and overcome evil with good.

We never have enough CARE packs

THE SEED IS IN THE FRUIT

PART XII

PART XII

Carl Mortenson, designer of *The Angel*, and I.
It is our hope and prayer that this magnificent aircraft
will soon be in service for the Lord in Colombia

CHAPTER 43

We all know the tragic story of the children of Israel who all went up to Mount Sinai after being delivered from bondage in Egypt. God gave them such a wonderful opportunity to hear His voice, yet because of the thunder and the lightning and the earthquake, they said, "We don't want to hear this voice any longer, because if we hear this voice any longer, we're going to die. Moses, would you please go up to the top of that mountain and listen to Him and come back and tell us, and we'll do whatever He says."

They thought that was a wonderful proposition for God, and God said that they spoke well what they spoke. But they went into 15 hundred years of law under which it was impossible for them to really be able to continue to move forward in victory as a nation. This happened because they did not realize that when you receive a second-hand word and revelation, it lacks the power and the provision

Marina and I unpack Galcom solar radios fix tuned to our frequencies

and the grace to accomplish the will and the purpose of God.

It is only in hearing His voice directly for ourselves that we can really have God's word and His will brought into reality in our lives. Yes, to continue to hear the voice of the Lord will definitely cost us our own life; but Jesus wants us to be Born Again into His life.

So if we think that it's a safer bet to have a leader who can hear from God and tell us, things will eventually turn into a miserable mess. And the true leadership ordained by God understands that the role of a leader is a servant role, so that the people might be joined to the Lord and remain joined to the Lord. God-ordained leadership is to help facilitate the personal relationship of each and every one to the Lord and then to watch and help make sure that that personal relationship with the Lord remains intact and to sound an alarm if that personal relationship with the Lord is ever endangered.

This is the main purpose of the ministry. The main purpose of the ministry is not to think up plans or projects. It is not to get people to do things. It is not to try and solve people's problems, although sometimes ministry ends up doing all kinds of things that if the people were really in touch with the Lord, the ministry wouldn't have to do.

Moses got overloaded with all the difficulties of having to judge the problems and conflicts of the people, and God had to multiply the spirit that was in Moses into other leadership to be able to handle the load. The prophetic ministry got started as a result of the people not wanting to hear from God on their own.

That's what the Scripture says in the book of Deuteronomy.

And God said, "Okay, if they don't want to hear My voice that's fine, but I'm going to send someone to tell them, and if they don't listen, they are going to be held responsible."

Literature ready for distribution

That's essentially what He said. And of course the key prophet who was sent was the Lord Jesus Christ.

Revelation 19:10 says that "the testimony of Jesus is the spirit of prophecy".

And people who don't understand that think

there is a gift of prophecy that they can exercise in and of themselves and be a "prophet".

The real prophetic ministry is Jesus speaking in and through people like you and me, who choose to give priority to His words and to His life rather than our own.

When God saw fit to multiply what was in Moses, there were two guys who were on the list that God had given, who didn't make it to the meeting. When the Holy Spirit touched the ones that were separated out for leadership, these two fellows, who were still down at the camp, started prophesying in the camp, while all the others were up at the Tabernacle. When young Joshua said, "Eldad and Medad are down there in the camp prophesying, Stop them!" What did Moses respond? Moses said he would that all God's people might prophesy. (See Numbers Chapter 11).

Eldad means "God is a friend" and Medad means "love".

And so God's plan is not to have a small elite group of people in ministry who lord it over everybody else and who have an inside track with God. God's plan is to have friends who flow in His love who will grow to maturity in Christ, due to direct contact with Him.

It is His right and His privilege to be able to delegate responsibility and leadership as He sees fit. But leadership in the kingdom of God is different from leadership in the world that surrounds us. The Lord said that the leadership in His kingdom means that the one who is the greatest is really the one that is the servant of all. It is the one willing to put his shoulder under the load and take the responsibility.

Working on the airplane

Those that God chose for leadership were like King David. When he was a little boy he was out taking care of the sheep instead of horsing around in town. He was willing to risk his own life for the sheep if he thought there was a threat or if a lion or a bear showed up.

God liked that, and He said, "This little David, he's a man after my own heart."

So He anointed him to be king and shepherd over the whole nation of Israel.

He didn't say, "Now, we're going to go down and see who the best student is down at the Tabernacle under the ministry of Samuel."

He didn't even say that young David had to be "trained"; God just had him come in from among the sheep and anointed him.

I'm told that when you anointed people back in those days, it was a horn full of oil, and if they made the whole formula according to Exodus Chapter 30, it made exactly two gallons of anointing oil. So when

Samuel poured two gallons of oil over the top of David's head, King David knew he had been anointed. He may have been remembering that experience when he wrote Psalm 133.

It wasn't like one of these deals today that a "little dab will do ya." It was an anointing that gave King David a supernatural ability to represent God among the people. He was able to not only kill lions or bears that were after the sheep, but he was able to kill giants that were after his brothers.

David was able to learn, however, that the anointing God gives has to be placed back at the feet of the Lord and used exclusively under the guidance of the Holy Spirit. King Saul never understood this. When the Holy Spirit left Saul, he did not even notice.

My dad, who is also a pilot,
has taught me a lot

CHAPTER 44

Some very interesting sacrifices are described in the book of Leviticus. There is a peace offering; there is a daily sacrifice, morning and evening. The symbolic plan of the Gospel in Leviticus starts out by sacrificing cattle that are representative of us in the flesh, bound by sin and corruption. And the very thing that God wanted sacrificed got inverted when they went off the rails. They made a golden calf and started worshipping the sin that God wanted dead in their lives. This is the root of humanism. God wants us dead to sin. Humanism exalts, dignifies and even deifies sin.

The next thing God wants to kill is our guilt represented in Leviticus by a he goat that must be brought under control, bled to death, and burned on the altar of God, (In the Old Testament, the word for "sheep" or "small cattle" can apply to either sheep or goats, because under the law, you can handle either one. It is not until the New Testament that a clear cut division is made between the "sheep" and the "goats".)

There is another very interesting number pattern, in that there are 276 verses in the Bible that have the word *sheep* or *small cattle*. In the Old Testament, the daily sacrifice, morning and evening at the tabernacle, could be either a sheep or a goat, but in the New Testament, Jesus says that the day will come when He is going to judge between the sheep and the goats. People can think that they're in the flock, but we can be in the flock as a sheep or we can be in the flock as a goat. The nature of the two animals is very different.

In the end, the Lord is going to separate them out, just the same as He is going to separate out the tares from the wheat. It is essentially the same example. Under law, you can control the goats. In fact it takes law, harshly, rigidly applied in order to control goats. And lots of leaders get into such a fixation on the goats that they start mistreating the sheep. Then the sheep get upset and start leaving. There are clergy that end up with a whole flock of goats, which would be essentially the same as having a bundle of tares.

A few years ago I was preaching in northern Canada about the difference between the "sheep" and the "goats" and the need to be Born Again. After the service, a little-six-year-old girl came up to the front and spoke with me.

She said, "I think I understood your message, Mr. Stendal. Now I know why they call us *kids*!"

Towards the end of the book of Acts, Paul told

the ship captain and the centurion that it would not be wise to sail, and they did anyway. In this example, I believe that the ship is a symbol of the church

These little friends have helped distribute many radios

led by man, and Paul is a symbol of the Holy Spirit. There are a lot of churches that want to have "Paul" on board, but they have him in chains, and when he says what needs to be done, they think they know better.

There were 276 souls on board this particular ship, and when they went through the "judgment" (storm), they finally started listening to Paul. The Original says that when they got scared and started to lighten ship, that on the third day "they cast off the dead works of the ship" (Acts 27:19).

The ship came apart, but the people were saved, and that is God's plan in the end. The structures built by men are not going to make it through the Day of the Lord that is coming. But God does want the people saved if they will listen to what the Holy Spirit is saying in this hour. And just like the example of the sheep and the goats, there are also 276 verses in the Bible that use the word *judgment*.

In the King James Bible, and in the previous

editions that led up to it, the Bible translators back in the Reformation, starting with William Tyndale and those after him, placed special attention on words like *judgment*. The King James Bible has the word *judgment* in about 285 verses, if I can remember right, because translators put it in a few times in italics just to make sure that you wouldn't misunderstand other passages. But by the time we get to our RSV Bible, it went down to 180 some times and then by the time you get to the NIV Bible, there are only 121 or so verses with the word *judgment* left because many of our modern scholars don't like that word.

As I have already mentioned, in the Bible, the word, *sheep*, starting with the small cattle, which can be either sheep or goats that were used for the morning and evening sacrifice (you could sacrifice either one in the Temple), then on through to the distinction of *sheep* as we know it in the New Testament, is in exactly 276 verses. And that is what God's judgment is going to be about.

There are going to be those who, because of the nature of the life of Christ in them, were doing what was pleasing to God without even fully realizing it.

They are the ones in the end when the Lord says to them, "Enter in at my right hand, to the kingdom, because when I was hungry you fed me, when I was thirsty you gave me something to drink, when I was in prison, and when I was sick, you visited me."

"Well Lord, we don't remember doing that to you."

But they did it to the right people and at the right time because the very nature of God was m o v i n g them. Then, you have these other people that

Policemen receive us and our materials

thought they were part of the flock because somebody had herded them into the corral. But they did their own thing at their own time. They may have "helped" all kinds of people but they didn't help those who God wanted helped, and they missed it.

The people that are living their own life and trying to use God to make the most of their own life are going to be separated off from the ones that are willing to sacrifice their own lives in order to live God's life. This is what it is going to come down to in the end.

These patterns are all over Scripture. I am not basing doctrines on a verse here or a verse there; it is a consistent pattern throughout the entire Bible. The work of our hands, if it does not flow as the result of a blood covenant with God, is totally unacceptable to God, even if it looks like a "good" work to us. A blood covenant means a change of life. This is why the Gospel clearly states that we must be *Born Again* from above.

CHAPTER 45

God wants to move us from the inside. In many biblical examples, He has had to work with His people through different levels of maturity. We have heard a lot of teaching on the difference between little children and young men and fathers, but what God wants to accomplish in our lives is to bring us to a place of maturity in Christ.

God wants us to have such a change of heart that we are being led by God's heart. Then we can discern the difference between God's feelings and our feelings, between God's thoughts and our thoughts.

He has placed ministry along the way to help us sort things out. The best success that I've had in ministry is when God was dealing with somebody, and all I had to do was explain to them what God was doing, rather than me trying to be God and attempt to direct somebody else's life. At best that will only work for a very short time and season, and it's a very dangerous thing to do.

As we come through the book of Leviticus, we begin to see that the Gospel is there, complete, in the book of Leviticus. It's there throughout all the books of Moses. Paul in the New Testament said that when Moses was read to the Jews, they could not understand it, because there was a veil over their hearts. So it is not something that will be understood intellectually, it is something that unless God removes the veil from our hearts, we can't understand the real message.

We have people in many Christian churches who even though they read the New Testament and study it with great fervor, they still have the veil over their hearts, and they don't really understand what God is after. They don't realize how deep He really wants to go. They think that He's still trying to rehabilitate Adam, when God's plan is to do away with Adam, the old man, so that Jesus Christ, the new man can live in us.

False religion always wants to kill Jesus (the new man) so that Barabbas (the old man) can live. So as we go through the book of Leviticus, we begin to see that God really wants a priesthood of all believers, a kingdom of priests. In His dealings with the children of Israel, taking them out of Egypt, bringing them through the desert and entering them into the Promised Land is a type and a shadow of what God wants to do with all of His people.

God wants to bring us out from under the bondage to sin and the devil and the world, lead us through the wilderness of our own "good" intentions and bring us into the fullness of our inheritance in Jesus Christ.

But He doesn't take us right out from under "Pharaoh" and put us directly into the "Promised Land" because we can't handle that. And so what He did was He ran them around in the wilderness until He had dealt with a whole unbelieving generation at the same time as He was raising up a generation that really did believe Him.

To believe in Him is not just a head knowledge of believing historical facts about Him. Believing in Him means to depend on Him and to depend on His life and not on our own life. When God gave the law the first time, He wrote it on tablets of stone after the children of Israel had said that they didn't want to hear His voice for themselves.

They sent Moses to hear from God instead. And Moses was coming down the mountain, after 40 days on top of the mountain with the two tablets of stone, and before he even got to camp, he realized that they'd broken just about every commandment.

Our little friends love to listen to our childrens radio programs. There is no TV in these areas

CHAPTER 46

Everything was totally out of control down in the camp. Moses threw the tablets down, and they broke. Then Moses spent another 40 days fasting and praying so that God wouldn't destroy the people. Then He went up the mountain and spent another 40 days fasting to get the law the second time. If you add it all up, Moses fasted 120 days which is humanly impossible. In order to get our human situation all straightened out, it is humanly impossible. It's not possible for *us* to get this straightened out on our own.

But the Lord is very interested in straightening it out and in straightening us out. So when the law was given the second time, God said, "Make an ark." This is called the Ark of the Covenant or the Ark of the Testimony (or witness). And in the New Testament, witness means Martyr (those willing to lay down their lives for the truth). The new tablets were not just to be delivered over to the people. They were to be placed beyond the reach of those who wanted to conserve their own life and not hear directly from God. They were placed in the Ark of the Covenant within the Holy of Holies.

The people of Israel under the Old Covenant could only get as far as the outer court; they could get to the altar and bring their sacrifice, which was to be their sin, their guilt or the peace offering, which was to be themselves cleansed from sin and guilt. Then God transitioned their worship into offering sheep, which symbolize the new nature in Christ. The sacrifice of Jesus Christ is an example that we are encouraged to follow. Paul speaks of us being crucified with Christ.

Even when we receive the salvation and life of God in the form of the down payment of the Holy Spirit, after we are set free from sin, the world and the Devil, what is really pleasing to God is if we voluntarily offer ourselves back to Him. This is the way to really come into the fullness of His plan and purpose. There are certain things that are obligatory; there are other things that must be done on a free-will basis.

God wants to see what it's going to be in our lives. There are things that are required, and there are other things that are not required. God wants to see what we're going to do with whatever blessing He gives us. God knew that the people under the Old Covenant were not going to be able to fulfill the law and from the very beginning He wrote it in future tense. He didn't say, "Don't do that, Don't do this." He said, "Thou shalt not…"

God knew it wasn't going to work at the time, but the Ten Commandments are a prophecy that there would come a time when this desire of God was going to be implemented in and through people like us.

This guerrilla girl wants a radio and a book

He had the second set of stone tablets put in the Holy of Holies, in the Ark of the Covenant, (the Ark of the Testimony, the Ark of the Witness), the Ark that symbolizes us dead to sin and Jesus alive in us. The Ark has a seat on the top of it that mistakenly was translated *mercy seat* by William Tyndale. But the word *mercy* is not in the Hebrew; it is the root word, *reconciliation*, which means being lined up straight and true, even as God is straight and true, so that we will be compatible with God. Reconciliation does not mean meeting God halfway, somewhere between His righteousness and our corruption.

The seat of reconciliation is the place where we can get lined up straight again with God. If we attempt to come into the "Holy of Holies" in our own life, we won't survive, because no one can enter back into the presence of God in their own life and live. The provision has been made that we can come back to the presence of God in the life of Jesus Christ. And in that Ark of the Testimony (of the Witness, of being a martyr), which means standing up for the truth to the point of being willing to lay down our own life, it is a special provision of God only available to those who have been reconciled to Him in Jesus Christ.

If we come back to God under these conditions, Jesus will apply the truth, because He is our new high priest and He mediates the New Covenant now. He will pour His life into us through the Holy Spirit. He will apply the truth with the fire of His love. In the Ark of the Covenant is a golden pot with the hidden manna, which is the provision from God to bring us through the wilderness of the "good" intentions of our own life and of our own self and into the fullness of His life.

In the Ark of the Covenant is the rod of "Aaron" (Aaron means *illuminated*) that budded and bore fruit, which is God's discipline upon us as His sons, not to destroy us, but to bring forth the fruit of the Holy Spirit in us. (When God speaks of us as His sons, this is not gender sensitive, because in Christ there is neither male nor female). This rod didn't just bud, it didn't just blossom, it bore fruit.

He put it all there in the "Ark" as a symbol that there was going to be a period of time under the law in which God's people were not going to be able to do it; it would be beyond their reach. There was going to be a time in the "Holy Place" of ministration as priests (the priesthood of all believers) under the Age of Grace, the Age of the Church, and that as long as mankind continued to impose their own "good" ideas, they were not going to completely fulfill the commandments of God, either.

Even with such wonderful gifts of God's grace as found in the Holy Place: The "golden lamp stand" of the written Word of God for daily

Many lives are being touched

devotions, the "showbread" of communion in our corporate gatherings, the "golden altar of incense" allowing each person born again into the priesthood of all believers to have direct contact through prayer with the throne of God; even so, the people were not going to be able to completely fulfill the law of God within this realm.

Jesus's death at Calvary rent the veil between the Holy Place and the Holy of Holies, but men soon sewed it back up. For almost two millennia, some, like the Pharisees of old, have made an all out effort to turn the New Covenant back into an Old Covenant of man-contrived doctrines, principles and regulations, administered by an intermediary clergy positioned between the people and God. In the Age of Grace, God has not ruled out our input. He has allowed the consequences of all our "good" ideas to be made manifest over almost two thousand years of human history since Jesus Christ walked the earth.

But He is also planning to return for a bride

These guerrillas and many others are faithful listeners of our radio stations

without spot or wrinkle or any such thing. And those commandments that were written as a prophecy in the books of Moses continue to become real in the heart of the believer, as Jesus continues to mediate the New Covenant.

Seated at the right hand of the Father with all power and authority, Jesus can inscribe the will of God on the "tablets" of our hearts, in our souls, and in our minds. The commandments locked in the "Ark" of his heavenly tabernacle (of which Moses only made a copy) are being fulfilled in a people that have been reconciled back into His life.

If we plant a fruit tree of a good variety and take good care of it, and we have a wonderful apple tree that produces wonderful, delicious apples out in the backyard, we don't have to go show it an apple and say, "you have to make the apples just like this and make sure you get the color right..."

We don't have to do anything like that. If it has the right life and if it's well cared for, the natural thing is going to be to produce those wonderful apples. No one has to train it to make wonderful apples, nobody has to tell it to make them this size and not that size, or this color and not this other color, it is a direct result of the life that is well taken care of from that seed that will eventually bear that result.

If the life of the Lord Jesus really comes into us, and if we demonstrate in daily life that our priority is His life and not our own life, He promises that He will complete the work that He has begun in us, and we will bear the fruit of the Holy Spirit *and the seed is in the fruit*.

So if we are out trying to evangelize people into the kingdom of God, and we are not bearing the fruit of the Holy Spirit, we haven't got any incorruptible seed to plant in any one else's life. This is why so many attempts at evangelism have failed. According to the New Covenant, we are to be the seed that God wants to plant.

With my close friend and mentor, Clayt Sonmore, whom God has used greatly in Colombia

Epilogue

Newsletter, October, 2007

We have recently made some trips into the vast Colombia Venezuela border area where it appears that a major storm is brewing. Evangelical Christians are coming under increasing pressure. Venezuela is implementing extreme socialistic reforms with the help of thousands of foreign advisors, including many from Cuba and Iran. Colombia is in an all out war against guerrillas and drug traffickers with help from the US and her allies. Right wing illegal paramilitary forces are also operating on both sides of the border. Christians who refuse to get involved in politics or violence are often persecuted by all sides.

Young people who have Christian parents are being forcibly recruited into illegal terrorist groups; some who refused were reportedly shot and killed. In addition to Marxist guerrillas and rightist paramilitary groups, several Islamic groups such as

Hezbollah are reported to be operating within the Venezuela border area.

Most churches and pastors seem unprepared for what is coming. Masses of individuals and groups are siding with the Venezuelan government and others are strongly opposed. No one is sure about whom they can trust. Pastors say that those who refuse to allow their church buildings to be used for political purposes are being threatened and that churches are being forced to pay money to political groups and even to terrorist groups. Leaders who refuse are being harassed, and some have even been murdered.

In the midst of all the turmoil, there are ever-increasing opportunities for the Gospel. Throughout history persecution has never been able to stop Christianity. We feel that now is the time to do the most that we can to spread the Gospel into this very needy and critical area. Pray that we will have the finances to operate our new Cessna 180 so that we can continue to fly into remote places that have not seen a missionary or a Bible for many years or ever.

We are making plans to beef up our radio transmitters and to make a new short wave transmitter which will target this area. Thousands of Bibles are also needed. We are planning a new FM repeater on top of a very high mountain. Pray that we will have the necessary resources.

Several weeks ago I sent a copy of a recent movie about Martin Luther to Noel (the guerrilla unit commander on the back cover of this book). This film showed how Martin Luther won the day with a pen instead of a sword. I sent word that this was the kind of peaceful revolution that we are interested in. Noel watched the movie, and then replied that he was in agreement. He said, "If this is what you want to do, you can count on me!" Now we are allowed to freely distribute our radios and Bibles to the people in many areas.

In our convention on October 31 it was brought to our attention that this date started out as All Saints Day. Then, on October 31, 1517 it became Martin Luther Day or Reformation Day when Martin Luther nailed the 95 Theses on the door of the church at Wittenberg. It is an unparalleled travesty that this has nearly been forgotten and twisted into Halloween! It is our earnest hope and prayer that what was begun 490 years ago in the Reformation will be continued here in Colombia until the Glory of the Lord shall cover and flow out from this nation and the world over.

The Angel airplane project is coming along nicely. We now have almost one third of the cost of this magnificent aircraft which will greatly enhance our ability to get the job done. This airplane has double the capacity of our Cessna 180 and is able to safely fly over the jungles and mountains and at night and in bad weather. It is crucial for this project to be financed so that we can spread the message further. You can obtain further information at: www.angelaircraft.com

Newsletter, November, 2007

We were able to fly into the town of Puerto Boyaca, bastion of the paramilitary forces, and begin distribution of Bibles, radios and other materials. Meanwhile we also continue to follow up leads and open doors into the Macarena mountains where many guerrillas continue to hide out. The Lord has granted us great favour to work with all the different sides.

Two weeks ago I got an urgent phone call from the army general in charge of the area around our Lomalinda radio station. A twin-engine turbine airplane with a full load of soldiers had gone down in the mountains, and I was asked to help with the search and rescue. Even though the ELT (emergency locator beacon) on the aircraft was not functioning, I was able to determine the general location of the crash (not far from the airplane crash that I helped find two years ago when the Lord helped me find Maria).

I took a team of men, including some converted, former guerrillas, up into the high mountains for ten days. We found some trails and camps abandoned years ago by the guerrillas and were able to get up into the general area of the accident. Then a government aircraft spotted the wreckage more or less where I thought it would be, and helicopters were sent in. Unfortunately there were no survivors as the plane hit directly into the side of a cliff at almost eleven thousand feet above sea level.

The good thing that happened was that we were able to find a viable way to get back up to a beautiful glacial lake with a waterfall, where I have been contemplating a high mountain FM repeater that will be able to reach most of southeast Colombia with the Gospel. I was amazed that the entire area has been abandoned by both the paramilitary and the guerrillas, and now it seems that the Lord has left this magnificent area as an inheritance for us.

On the lower slopes of the mountains *campesino* coffee farmers listen with great interest to our radio stations. In an area with no TV, many of the children listen without fail to our special youth programs. Most everyone is willing to help us in any way they can to increase our radio coverage.

Now we are in the midst of opening good trails to the site of the projected FM repeater. We must haul large quantities of eight inch PVC pipe and many rolls of electrical wire, as well as the tower, antennas, transmitter and water-powered Pelton generator. It took us five days to hike up the mountain and three days to come back down. We will have to spend thousands of hours of work to cut these times in half and to be able to get a mule trail at least part way up. Cabins will have to be built in strategic locations along the way. Severe winds and sub zero temperatures are normal at these high altitudes.

This project is a massive undertaking for us with extremely high stakes. If successful, we will be able to put a clear FM stereo signal into the worst part of the Colombian war zone and even have an impact into the volatile border areas of Venezuela, Brazil, Peru and Ecuador. One repeater on the top of this huge mountain will have more coverage than 100 normal stations. The financial hurdles, however, are also quite high, but not insurmountable.

I recently came across this quote:

"It is not the critic who counts; not the man who points out how the strong man stumbled, or where the doer of deeds could have done them better. The credit belongs to the man who is actually in the arena, whose face is marred by dust and sweat and blood; who errs and comes short again and again; who knows the great enthusiasms, the great devotions; who spends himself in a worthy cause; who, at the best, knows in the end the triumph of high achievement, and who, at the worst, if he fails, at least fails while daring greatly, so that his place shall never be with those timid souls who know neither victory or defeat." Theodore Roosevelt, 26th US President.

The greatest blessing we have is the growing throng of converts who are willing to risk their lives and go all out to help promote the cause of Christ.

Afterword

November, 2007

*T*he primary focus of this book has not been a comprehensive account of our life and ministry over the past couple decades, but rather the ongoing story of what God has been doing with the guerrillas who captured me 24 years ago. For one reason or another many exciting details must be left out. There are many ongoing testimonies which we are unable to relate at this time, but maybe later on.

There are also legal factors which complicate things. For instance, the Patriot Act, which contains important stipulations and safeguards for the security of our country, does not appear to contemplate or to include provision for missionaries to contact and relate to terrorists or terrorist organizations for the purpose of evangelizing them. I encourage our lawmakers to amend this law, and to make explicit provision for unlimited missionary activity. In the ongoing war against terrorism the Gospel is the deciding factor. If those whose hearts are hard and bitter are converted by the love of

Jesus Christ, they will no longer participate in any terrorist activity.

We make every effort to comply with the laws of the United States and Colombia and their spirit so that our mission effort will in no way aid or abet any illicit activities of terrorists or anyone. As the Gospel spreads from one individual to the next, it actually has the effect of thwarting diabolical plans for terror and violence. These are stories that are also difficult for us to share at this time because we do not want those who are still dedicated to violence and terror to retaliate against us or others.

The events recorded in this book are true to the best of my knowledge and recollection, and in most cases the people who are mentioned have given permission for their names to be used. All of the names are correct except when the initial use is in quotations " " which denote that the name has been changed for security or other reasons.

We are hoping that many of you will continue to pray for us and for all of those who are named in this book. We urgently need support. It will make a difference. You may contact us through our mission offices in Canada and in the United States.

**Tax Deductible donations
may be sent via:**

**Pan America Mission Inc.
P.O. Box 429, Newburg, Oregon, USA,
97132-0429**

**Colombia Para Cristo Society,
12629 – 248th St.,
Maple Ridge, BC,
Canada V4R 1K4**